JB JOSSEY-BASS™
A Wiley Brand

T0327705

Member Benefits

96 Benefits and Services That Attract and Retain Members

Scott C. Stevenson, Editor

WILEY

978-1-118-69198-4   ISBN

978-1-118-70409-7   ISBN (online)

Member Benefits:
96 Benefits and Services That Attract, Retain Members

Published by

Stevenson, Inc.

P.O. Box 4528 • Sioux City, Iowa • 51104
Phone 712.239.3010 • Fax 712.239.2166
www.stevensoninc.com

TABLE OF CONTENTS

TABLE OF CONTENTS

—— Member Benefits: 96 Benefits and Services That Attract, Retain Members ——

1. Do You Offer Member Add-ons?

Would your organization benefit by offering add-ons to different membership levels?

Add-ons are a way to enhance membership levels by providing exclusive benefits.

Many museums offer additional incentives, or add-ons, to keep members engaged.

Rachel C. Mentink-Ferraro, manager, general membership, Dallas Museum of Art (Dallas, TX), says the museum's add-on categories, in place since 2003, are so popular that some 60 percent of eligible members take advantage of the options.

"The categories give members a chance to become more involved with the museum while meeting other members who have similar interests, and allowing them to deepen their interest in a particular area of art," says Mentink-Ferraro. "For the museum, the add-on categories serve as a great way to upgrade members who are interested in joining these groups, while helping us strengthen our membership base."

At the Dallas Museum of Art, the add-on groups are built into the membership levels. Mentink-Ferraro explains how they work:

❑ **Members at Sustainer Level ($125) or higher can choose two of these groups:**

  1. **Encore!** —This group receives exclusive invitations and reserved seating for special events and discounts on performing arts and music-related programs in the museum and community;

  2. **Kids Club** — Kids Club is a partnership between the museum, Dallas Zoo, Museum of Nature and Science, Dallas Children's Theater and Trinity Audubon Center. By joining at any of these organizations, families receive special benefits from all five, including exclusive invitations to club-only events throughout the year at each institution and admission discounts at partnering institutions; and

  3. **Professional Members League** — This group gives working professionals the chance to meet other working professionals, become involved in the Dallas arts community and help the museum through volunteer work. Members enjoy special art education programs, exclusive events to meet other members and participate together as museum volunteers.

❑ **Any member at the Friend Level ($250) or higher may select one of the following groups:** Friends of Modern and Contemporary Art, Friends of Fine and Decorative Art, and Friends of World Art and Archaeology. Members of these groups enjoy curator-led programs and lectures throughout the year while getting to know fellow members who share their interest in a particular area of art.

Staff promote add-ons through membership material, membership sales, upgrades, word-of-mouth and the website. Eligible members who have not chosen groups are urged in mailings to take advantage of this benefit, says Mentink-Ferraro, who says they are considering add-ons to upper general membership levels such as the $500 level.

Source: Rachel C. Mentink-Ferraro, Manager, General Membership, Dallas Museum of Art, Dallas, TX.
Phone (214) 922-1212. E-mail: RFerraro@DallasMuseumofArt.org

2. Alternative Membership Dues, Benefits Boost Young Members

The staff at the Colorado Association of Libraries (CAL), Lakewood, CO, has found a way to meet the needs of their youngest members when it comes to paying their dues.

Jody Howard, president, says they have structured their membership fees, in a sense, based on prospective members' ability to pay.

People may join the association through one of seven levels based primarily on income or salary level. Students, retirees and people not actively working in the library profession pay $45 a year, while those making $60,000-plus a year pay $120 for membership.

The system uses an honor policy, not asking for proof of salary.

Younger members also benefit by being matched with mentors, pairing up with more accomplished professionals to present at conferences and getting discounts to attend professional conferences. The organization also offers scholarships for conference attendance and continuing education.

Howard says that while emphasis is placed on helping the younger members out, the association more than benefits from their generosity as members go up the scale.

"As members move up, they are expected to start giving back by being on committees and becoming mentors themselves," Howard says, "and most are happy to do this as they have seen the benefit in their own careers."

Source: Jody K. Howard, President, Colorado Association of Libraries, Thornton, CO. Phone (303) 859-1242.
E-mail: jodyhoward@comcast.net

3. Chamber Offers Varied Networking Opportunities

Are you offering your members various networking opportunities? Create a yearlong calendar of networking events. Here are opportunity examples offered by the Jacksonville Regional Chamber of Commerce (Jacksonville, FL):

1. **Network Now** — Host a quarterly seminar facilitated by a professional trainer who provides members with proper networking techniques to gather the most information from events.

2. **Five-minute Networking** — Offer this unique networking event quarterly to provide members a chance to network in a structured environment. Similar to speed-dating, this event offers members the opportunity to network with each other one-on-one in five-minute intervals.

3. **IMPACTjax** — A program specifically targeting young professionals. The program provides young men and women just starting out a venue to network with one another and a chance to get connected in their community and develop personally and professionally.

Source: Janelle Behr, Senior Manager, Marketing and Communications, Jacksonville Regional Chamber of Commerce, Jacksonville, FL. Phone (904) 366-6681. E-mail: Janelle.Behr@MyJaxChamber.com

4. 'E-Decal' Benefits Member Organization, Members

Chambers of Commerce have long provided members with chamber identification for promotional purposes. The Greater Wilmington Chamber of Commerce (Wilmington, NC) takes that idea a step further by offering an e-decal — a specially designed version of the standard chamber logo — that members may use on their websites and in communications supporting electronic graphics.

"Our new members always get a sticker to put on their door or window," says Scott Czechlewski, director of communications. "This is just a way to put that same logo on a website or e-mail."

The e-decal is available free to all member organizations. Interested persons simply fill out an online user agreement stipulating that they will not change or alter the logo. They then receive the logo in electronic format in three sizes in a JPEG image file format.

The e-decal is explained in member orientations, and Czechlewski estimates that one-fourth to one-third of all new members request it.

"It's particularly popular with smaller businesses or businesses that are new to the area," he says. "It's a way to show real involvement with the community. It also leverages the reputation and credibility of a well-respected organization seen to be the voice of the business community."

And the benefit to the chamber? "It's free publicity," Czechlewski says simply. The inexpensive member benefit "publicizes the services we offer to members and shows the strength we have in the community."

Source: Scott Czechlewski, Director of Communications, Greater Wilmington Chamber of Commerce, Wilmington NC. Phone (910) 762-2611 Ext. 216. E-mail: czechlewski@wilmingtonchamber.org. Website: http://wilmingtonchamber.sitewizard.biz/e_decal.html

5. Awards and Rewards Help Recruit and Retain Members

An awards program can serve to reward your existing members and garner attention to grow your membership base.

Staff at Associate Builders and Contractors, Inc. (ABC) headquartered in Arlington, VA, know the importance of recruiting and retaining members. To encourage recruitment and retention among members in its 78 chapters with a combined membership of more than 24,000 firms, staff developed an awards program offering incentives to members through the Beam Club.

Under the Beam Club, first established in 1966, ABC members are recognized for their commitment to grow the association by rewarding them with valuable gifts.

"ABC National supports the membership recruitment efforts of our chapters with our Beam Club program which recognizes members for their efforts," says Doug Curtis, vice president of chapter services. "We purchase and provide the awards so the chapters may recognize and reward members for their efforts. The awards are presented by the chapters."

Each member recruited is worth one point with points accruing year to year, advancing the member chapter to the next award level within the program. A member sponsor is enrolled in the Beam Club once five members are recruited.

Once 50 new members are recruited, the member receives national recognition by reaching the Beam Club Hall of Fame, with his/her name placed on the Hall of Fame plaque and chapter profiled in ABC's weekly electronic newsletter.

Club awards include plaques, lapel pins, shirts, jackets, watches, mantel clocks and more.

Source: Doug Curtis, Vice President of Chapter Services, Associate Builders and Contractors, Inc., Arlington, VA. Phone (703) 812-2009. E-mail: curtis@abc.org. Website: www.abc.org

6. Member Mixers Offer Multiple Benefits

Member mixers offer members a great way to network with each other and other local businesses.

"They are such a popular event we have our member mixers booked two years in advance," says Beth Morrison, vice president of member services, Dalton-Whitfield Chamber of Commerce (Dalton, GA).

Morrison says because member mixers can also be valued by local businesses, they have structured guidelines in place before contacting possible mixer locations so they know what to expect.

"At the beginning of each year, I send out two documents to each host site for that year," says Morrison. The documents include tips on invitations, posting greeters at specific locations, advertising, etc.

Carrie Stuart, director of membership, Gettysburg Adams Chamber of Commerce (Gettysburg, PA), says members are the hosts of their organization's mixers. "Only members are offered the opportunity to host a mixer. We leave it up to them what they would like to offer (e.g., door prizes, food, beverages, etc.). Once they have signed up for a mixer, we provide a letter with specific details and a checklist."

"Mixers allow members a valuable opportunity to showcase their business, service or product. It also provides members the ability to meet fellow members and establish business contacts in an informal setting," says Stuart.

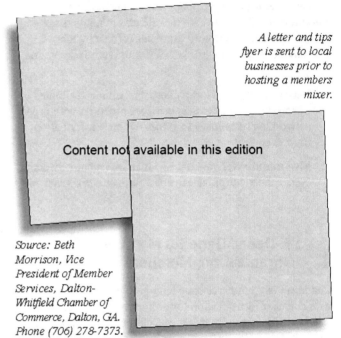

A letter and tips flyer is sent to local businesses prior to hosting a members mixer.

Content not available in this edition

Source: Beth Morrison, Vice President of Member Services, Dalton-Whitfield Chamber of Commerce, Dalton, GA. Phone (706) 278-7373. E-mail: morrison@daltonchamber.org
Carrie Stuart, Director of Membership, Gettysburg Adams Chamber of Commerce, Gettysburg, PA. Phone (717) 334-8151. Website: www.gettysburg-chamber.org

7. Affiliate Memberships Offer Many Benefits

The Society for Nonprofit Organizations (SNPO) of Canton, MI, offers an affiliate membership plan that provides a group of individuals access to SNPO membership at a vastly discounted rate — just $15 per year per person.

An affiliate membership — essentially a bulk buying program — through SNPO allows a group of 25 or more individuals to access complete SNPO membership plus a full membership in Grant Station (www.grantstation.com) — which provides services that help nonprofits identify funding — at a significantly reduced rate.

Nearly 4,000 of SNPO's 6,000 members fall under the affiliate membership category.

"Our affiliate members are thrilled with the value that we offer and have seen great boosts to their membership numbers as a result," says Jason Chmura, membership director for SNPO. "We've also had a number of corporations who purchase this type of membership to thank their nonprofit clients."

On their own, individuals would pay more than $600 per year to become members of SNPO and Grant Station, but under the affiliate membership program, a group of 25 members would pay just $375 combined — a group savings of more than $14,000 per year.

"We're able to offer this affiliate membership at a discount because we don't have to process payments and membership applications for each individual, saving on administrative costs," says Chmura.

Chmura offers five tips to successfully implement an affiliate membership program at your nonprofit:

1. Look for ways to acknowledge your affiliates with every benefit.

2. Prepare your data entry process for uploading bulk records.

3. Provide flexible payment options to accommodate affiliate members.

4. Think broadly about how others could benefit from your products and/or services.

5. Remember to include smaller affiliates with growth potential.

Source: Jason Chmura, Membership Director, Society for Nonprofit Organizations, Canton, MI. Phone (734) 451-3582. E-mail: jchmura@snpo.org

8. Member Coupons Provide Increased Exposure

Consider posting member coupons on your website to increase exposure and traffic.

The Central Delaware Chamber of Commerce (Dover, DE) recently implemented a new member benefit, allowing members to create and list business-related coupons on its website. The coupons, which can only be created by chamber members and must be of a business nature, can be accessed and printed by anyone visiting the website, members and nonmembers alike.

Chamber staff created this feature to provide members with an easy and free way to spread the word about their business to the community, says Judy Diogo, president.

A Web design firm is currently fine-tuning the customized coupon template to allow members to upload coupon information, including company contact information, coupon specifics and logo. This information will be sent to chamber staff for review. Upon approval, all member coupons appear on the same page of the chamber's website for 30 days where they can be printed for use.

With the coupon template still in the works, chamber staff have only done a soft launch of the feature so far, asking a couple of members to create coupons as a test. Once the final version is up and running, Diogo says, they plan to start a full campaign, announcing the new feature on their website, in all advertising materials, solicitation materials and in the chamber newsletter.

Hopes are that most, if not all, chamber members will take advantage of the opportunity to increase exposure of their business, says Diogo, who notes, "We are really trying to make sure it serves our entire membership."

Source: Judy Diogo, President, Central Delaware Chamber of Commerce, Dover, DE. Phone (302) 678-0892. E-mail: jdiogo@cdcc.net

9. Celebrate Your Members With Monthly Birthday Parties

If most of your members are within a short drive of your organization's headquarters, celebrate their birthdays and give them an opportunity to mingle with one another with a monthly party.

Staff with the Center for Active Generations (Sioux Falls, SD) have hosted monthly birthday parties for members for more than 25 years, says Lisa Howard, program director.

"This is just one way we can say thank you and honor our members," Howard says. "People like to feel special and enjoy getting together with others to celebrate. It's a 'no brainer' for a membership organization to acknowledge these special days."

Offered the second Friday of every month, the parties begin at 2 p.m. and last an hour to an hour and a half. They are free to attend, and are held in the center's dining room. Attendance ranges from 130 to 180 persons, including members and their guests.

All members, not just those celebrating a birthday that month, are invited to the monthly parties. The center holds a new-member social the hour before the birthday parties to encourage new members to attend popular monthly events.

Members celebrating a birthday that month are announced at each party and given a special name tag to wear.

Center staff publicize the parties through their website and monthly newspaper/program guide. The newspaper/guide includes pictures from the previous month's party, names of all members celebrating a birthday that month and credits the party sponsor.

The birthday parties are sponsored by the Good Samaritan Communities of Sioux Falls. The organization provides the birthday cake and provides each birthday guest with a special cookie baked by the organization's nutrition department.

"It's a 'no brainer' for a membership organization to acknowledge these special days."

Party attendees have a chance to win door prizes, which include two $50 gift cards for a regional supermarket chain that are good for groceries or gas. All attendees' names are placed in a box to be drawn for the door prize.

A volunteer master of ceremonies and other volunteers serve the cake and check guests in at the door.

For entertainment, the parties typically feature chorus groups and drama clubs from local schools that perform free of charge.

Howard offers this advice to other member organizations thinking of hosting monthly birthday parties: "Keep it simple and keep it fun. Great entertainment is a plus and fun door prizes make the event attractive to members and guests. Also, keep the event at about an hour and a half."

Source: Lisa Howard, Program Director, The Center for Active Generations, Sioux Falls, SD. Phone (605) 336-6722. E-mail: LHoward@cfag.org

10. Include Tangible Benefits

Beyond the social or altruistic reasons for attending a member event, incorporate tangible benefits for attending:

- An autographed book
- Continuing education credits
- Membership dues discounts
- Useful seminars
- A photo with a celebrity
- Complimentary website listing or link

11. Member Benefit Idea

- Consider offering free or reduced-rate day trips for members who give at higher levels. Come up with a menu of ideas that fit your mission and programs, then involve your members in selecting those with the widest appeal.

12. Community Service Projects Involve, Motivate Members

Promote community service projects as a benefit for your members.

The Pi Beta Phi sorority has a tradition of involvement in community service and philanthropy, says Kyleigh Merritt, chair of philanthropy programs for Phoenix (AZ) Alumnae Club of Pi Beta Phi. The organization promotes the belief that members have an obligation to support their communities and enrich the lives of others.

"It's a benefit for our members to participate in these projects," Merritt says. "They look for these opportunities to help out in the community — it enhances their lives personally and professionally."

The club's most popular community service projects center on literacy, a long-time focus of Pi Beta Phi through its national commitment to literacy, she says, noting, "We're passionate about this cause, as parents, teachers and other professionals. All of our 200 club members can get behind these projects."

Both the alumnae and collegiate clubs in Phoenix have partnered with the Chrysalis Shelter, a domestic abuse shelter in Phoenix, to provide reading programs. The ultimate goal for members is working toward providing the shelter with a library, stocked with books donated by Pi Beta Phi.

Members held community book drives for donations to the library. They also offered a fundraiser through the collegiate club members, made care-study baskets for finals week and asked parents of college students about buying their daughters a basket to support the library project.

To accommodate members' busy schedules, Merritt says, the organization offers advance information on service projects. The alumnae club's executive board plans an annual calendar, and all of the events, including community service projects, are published in a membership booklet given to all members.

The organization uses a free Internet service, www.evite.com, to e-mail members invitations two weeks before every event. Members RSVP via this service as well.

"We provide many opportunities for our members to get involved in service projects," Merritt says. "Once they're in the organization, we encourage them to try one of our events.

Sampling of Community Projects

Kyleigh Merritt, philanthropy chairman, Phoenix Alumnae Club of Pi Beta Phi (Phoenix, AZ), offers examples of community projects hosted by the club:

- **Reading Angels Night:** Members read to children staying at a local domestic abuse shelter. Alumnae and collegiate clubs alternate weekly shifts.

- **Champions Are Readers (CAR):** The club tailored this national program by adopting third-grade classrooms at a local elementary school. Each February, volunteers visit the students and read aloud to them. They provide workbooks and other materials to the school.

- **Assistance League of Phoenix:** The organization's book club assists this program by recording "books on tape" to give to schools — an ideal project for a busy member who can make the recordings on her own time.

- **Crisis Nursery:** Members work to support children affected by domestic abuse living in this shelter, hosting a pumpkin party and donating time and supplies as needed.

Other member-supported projects include participation in the Susan G. Komen Race for the Cure, and Relay for Life for the American Cancer Society. The club also recruits more than 100 volunteers to work at the annual PGA golf tournament held in Phoenix. In turn, they earn scholarship money for collegiate club members.

These projects become an amazing retention tool. The members enjoy following through on the projects and with the people they meet too."

Source: Kyleigh Merritt, Philanthropy Chairman, Phoenix Alumnae Club of Pi Beta Phi, Phoenix, AZ. Phone (480) 227-8603. E-mail: philanthropy@phoenixpibetaphi.org

13. Say 'Thank You' With Special Member Perks

Do you recognize your corporate members' contributions with special perks?

The next time a corporation elects to open its checkbook to your organization, offer special incentives to express your gratitude.

The following are special corporate perks offered by member organizations:

Chrysler Museum of Art (Norfolk, VA)
Corporate Members Networking Reception — Twice a year, members are invited to a networking reception which corresponds with the museum's special exhibitions program. The evening includes welcoming remarks from the museum's director and corporate committee chair, information on upcoming museum programs and events, corporate sponsorship opportunities, a cocktail reception and a private tour of the special exhibit on display.

American Museum of Natural History (New York City, NY)
Free Employee Admission — This corporate benefit has become the museum's most popular level, says Lucia Yoo, assistant director of corporate relations. The benefit allows all corporate employees, plus up to five guests, to visit the museum free for one year.

Corporate Event Privilege — Corporate members can host one event annually in the museum's exhibition halls after public hours. Yoo says many corporations have become members because of their interest in hosting events at the museum.

The Metropolitan Museum of Art (New York City, NY)
Breakfast at the Met — For an additional fee of $5,000, members at the sponsor level ($15,000) and above can take advantage of this special corporate perk. The event provides a buffet breakfast for up to 40 guests followed by an invitation to visit the galleries prior to the museum opening to the public. A docent is also available at a minimal cost to further enrich the experience.

Host after-hours exhibition viewings — This perk is offered as a unique entertainment option for the museum's corporate members ($3,000 and above). The benefit provides up to 75 guests, including employees, clients and investors, private access to the galleries from 6 to 7 p.m.

Source: Sarah Higby, Senior Development Officer, Corporate Annual Programs, The Metropolitan Museum of Art, New York, NY. Phone (212) 570-3947.
Joanne Leese, Director of Membership, Annual Giving & Affiliate Groups, Chrysler Museum of Art, Norfolk, VA. Phone (757) 333-6294. E-mail: jleese@chrysler.org
Lucia Yoo, Assistant Director of Corporate Relations, American Museum of Natural History, New York, NY.

14. New Membership Benefit: Offer Career Guidance

Go beyond typical benefits to "wow" your members and watch membership grow.

The mission of the Association for Visual Arts (AVA) of Chattanooga, TN, is to promote, support and advocate for original visual art and artists. Membership benefits go beyond typical benefits, such as member discounts, to include career coaching, professional development and technology access and training.

"We have many members who are emerging artists who weren't taught to promote themselves as part of their degree," says Nanette Ramsey, associate director. "In light of that, we offer career development workshops and sessions to assist the artist."

With AVA membership, members receive:

- ❑ **Career Coaching** — Mark Bradley-Shoup, director of programs, holds a masters in fine arts and heads up one-on-one sessions with artist members to direct them toward their career goals. In these sessions, he helps artists determine where their work can best be exhibited, discusses the basics of the business and guides them in developing their resumes and portfolios.
- ❑ **Professional Development Workshops** — Professional artists conduct a series of one- to two-hour micro-workshops tailored to emerging artists' needs (e.g., "How to Write a Resume or Curriculum Vitae," "How to Write a Bio or Artist Statement" and "How to Best Document Artistic Works"). Micro-workshops are $5 for members and $15 for nonmembers. AVA keeps costs low by working with local presenters to avoid mileage and overnight fees and by hosting the events on site.
- ❑ **Professional Technology** — The AVA provides updated technology for members' use. "We're unveiling two significant facets by adding a digital media lab with 10 Mac workstations with all the latest software," says Bradley-Shoup. Plans are to offer classes on how artists can use technology to their advantage, including a "clean room" with cameras and lighting to photograph artwork for portfolios.

Offering professional guidance and development is easy for any organization that has professionals in its ranks willing to share information with members, says Ramsey.

Sources: Nanette Ramsey, Associate Director; Mark Bradley-Shoup, Director of Programs, Association for Visual Arts, Chattanooga, TN. Phone (423) 265-4282. E-mail: nramsey@avarts.org

15. Grow Membership With Valuable Tools, Customer Service

By providing valuable tools and staying on top of customer service, your membership numbers will grow.

Within 15 months, Bridgestar (Boston, MA) doubled its membership to 20,000. Carol Trager, director of communications and marketing, attributes that leap to providing valuable resources and reacting to member feedback.

The nonprofit sector is likely to require more than half a million new leaders in the next decade, Trager says. Bridgestar, which is an initiative of The Bridgespan Group, is committed to building a network and talent pool of people who work in business or government and are attracted to mission-focused work.

"In support of our mission, we provide talent-matching services, content and tools designed to help organizations build strong leadership teams and individuals pursue career paths as nonprofit leaders," Trager says.

Valuable Tools — Bridgestar's job board is considered one of the organization's most valuable resources. It's a free membership benefit and the viewing and posting has grown rapidly. Other valuable resources include workshops and seminars for hiring managers and senior executives interested in moving to roles in nonprofits. A monthly newsletter, *Leadership Matters*, is widely read and quoted.

"We recently introduced the first of a set of mini-sites dedicated to content and tools around functional roles, through which we hope to build new networks," Trager says.

"Our executive recruiting and advisory services are fee-based and demand continues to increase, thanks to the reputation we have built through our talent-matching work and other services."

Customer Service — Bridgestar responds to every request and inquiry promptly and has a feedback section on its website. The feedback is shared with the management team when it's something actionable, especially if it's a consistently heard comment.

"If it's within the realm of possibility to address the issue, we do," she says. "For example, we streamlined our registration process based on feedback."

Bridgestar solicits direct feedback from clients and attendees at programs. This feedback also is reviewed thoroughly and adjustments have been made to services and programs because of it.

"Our recruiters keep tabs on the market and provide another feedback loop to marketing and our knowledge team," she says. "For example, the development of the COO site came out of indications that demand for nonprofit COOs is growing and some research showing few widely accessible, centralized resources for those considering, in or hiring for the role."

Source: Carol Trager, Director, Communications and Marketing, Bridgestar/The Bridgespan Group, Boston, MA. Phone (617) 572-2833. E-mail: info@bridgestar.org

16. Members Learn Over Breakfast

Offer your members learning opportunities at breakfast meetings.

The La Crosse Area Chamber of Commerce (La Crosse, WI) co-hosts the Business Over Breakfast Series. "Early morning breakfast programs have been the most successful," says Janet Loeffler, program manager. "It's sometimes easier for a small business person to attend a morning program versus leaving at another time during the day."

Chamber members, including business owners and managers, and other professionals meet to discuss various topics, such as team building and improving communication. The effort has been ongoing since January 2001. Members meet from 7:30 to 8:45 a.m. at the Chamber office. The cost is $5 per person, which includes a continental breakfast and program materials.

Business Over Breakfast is held monthly September through May, with the exception of December. Due to its popularity, the November session has evolved into a half-day program on a topic of interest. Popular topics include marketing, sales and leadership development.

"The size of the sessions varies according to the time of year and topics," Loeffler says. "Attendance has ranged from 12 to 60 people but average attendance is around 20 to 30."

The organization has collaborated with local groups and their members to help make the program successful: Downtown Main Street Inc.; Service Corp of Retired Executives (SCORE); Western Technical College; and the University of Wisconsin-La Crosse Small Business Development Center.

The planning committee meets in June to set the program for the following year. Contacting presenters, sending out publicity and other duties is divided among members of all participating organizations.

"Evaluation forms are distributed at the conclusion of each session to get feedback for the presenters," Loeffler says. "There is also space on the form for topics of interest. This helps the planning committee with future program topics."

Source: Janet Loeffler, Program Manager, La Crosse Area Chamber of Commerce, La Crosse, WI. Phone (608) 784-4880. E-mail: jloeffler@centurytel.net

17. Intrigue Members With Highlighted Benefits

Are your members aware of all the benefits available to them? Emphasizing membership benefits individually can help your members utilize all benefits to the fullest.

Rachel Smith, associate vice president, membership, California Medical Association, (Sacramento, CA) explains. "We weren't promoting our affinity partners as well as we could, and it was translating to less business for the partner. Not many of our members were taking advantage of available benefits. A number of long-time members weren't even aware of the discount programs or benefits. By doing a weekly spotlight on one benefit, we can now link the benefit to news that has relevance to the members. Taking the time to focus on a single benefit makes it easier for our members to absorb the information." Highlighting benefits individually can also attract the attention of potential members as well.

The medical association has been highlighting member benefits since early 2006. The benefits are spotlighted on the organization's website, as well as in the "CMA Alert," the association's weekly newsletter (sent to members who opt in). "Staff developed a small 'spotlight' in our weekly publication that complemented the overall message," says Smith. "Each spotlight briefly states the name of the partner, the program offered, the discount amount and the contact."

Smith details the process of choosing which benefit to highlight, saying, "To date, the highlights have been generated randomly. However, to enhance this program, we are laying out a 12-month schedule that enables the membership/marketing staff to coordinate in advance with our partners. We've also built in flexibility for breaking events in the news or legislature or to coordinate a time-specific product or program offered by one of our partners."

Creating an easily adaptable schedule for highlighting specific benefits makes the process more efficient. "Staff put together an excel spreadsheet to schedule the benefit of the week, noting the partner, the date the article will run and a type of priority based on previously established support and participation by the partner organization. As things change, based on any particular news event, we can simply cut, paste and rearrange them," says Smith.

Source: Rachel D. Smith, Associate Vice President, Membership, California Medical Association, Sacramento, CA.
Phone (916) 551-2073. E-mail: rsmith@cmanet.org

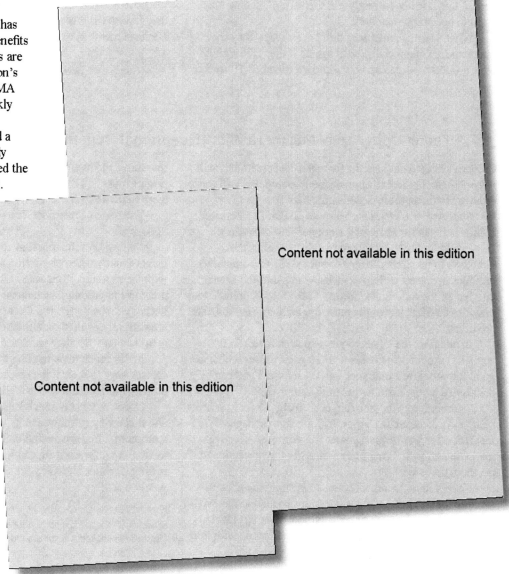

Content not available in this edition

Content not available in this edition

18. Boost Numbers With Free Child Memberships

Staff with the Sons of Norway (Minneapolis, MN) pride themselves on bringing Norwegian heritage and culture to their members. To help do so, they offer free Heritage memberships to children age 15 and younger with a relative who is a current member.

As many as 7,600 members fall into this special group.

Linda Nelson, fraternal manager, says the free membership is a win-win for the organization and young members.

"By introducing them to Sons of Norway, we get them interested in Norwegian heritage and culture at an early age," Nelson says. "This also assists in promoting membership to paying members by providing an added benefit of free membership to young relatives.

"Another benefit is that the parents of the Heritage members, if they are not currently members, may become interested in becoming members."

When Heritage members turn 16, she says, they may maintain free membership until age 23 if they live with or have a lineal relationship with a current member. Those age 16 to 23 without a lineal relative who is a current member can continue membership at half price.

All Heritage members receive the organization's award-winning quarterly Viking for Kids magazine and access to a self-paced cultural program with individual study units in topics such as folk dancing, weaving, genealogy and Norwegian cooking. Participants earn pins for every level completed. Youth members can also participate in a sports medal program, earning pins for being physically active.

Nelson says the Sons of Norway organization encourages individual lodges to participate at festivals in their local area and promote Heritage membership as a benefit. Information about the special membership option is included in promotional materials and in materials sent to all new members.

"Also, when we sign up a new adult member we ask if they have a child or grandchild they would like to enroll as a Heritage member," Nelson says.

Source: Linda Nelson, Fraternal Manager, Minneapolis, MN. Phone (612) 827-3611. E-mail: lnelson@sofn.com

19. Thank Upper-level Members With Exceptional Benefits

Creating exceptional benefits for upper-level members will not only tempt others to upgrade membership, but will serve as a way to thank these notable members.

Staff with the Women's Museum (Dallas, TX) created unique benefits for some of their upper-level members.

In addition to the standard member benefits, the director's inner circle membership level ($1,000 annually) provides members with invitations to a behind-the-scenes tour led by the museum's director. The 60- to 90-minute tour provides an overview of the museum, including exhibits and programs.

In addition, the silver corporate patron level ($5,000 annually) provides members with 30 guest passes which are good for one-time admittance into the museum and can be distributed by the member to family and friends.

"Admission to the museum is normally $5 for nonmembers," says Mackenzie Causey, membership manager. "We feel that offering the guest passes is a very cost effective marketing effort to bring more visitors to the museum and get them involved."

Causey says the organization added more benefits to some of their upper- level memberships so that donors would see the added value to their contribution. "Our top-level memberships provide a more intimate relationship with the museum," the membership manager says. "For example, our private tours and free guest passes for our members allow them to invite their closest friends."

The benefits mentioned above have been offered since 2000.

Causey says the museum showcases all membership levels equally when promoting membership opportunities with the museum. "Because of the high number of our members upgrading, we believe our membership levels have been well received," says Causey. "With that being said, we are currently evaluating our levels and plan to survey our members on what they want and feel is a valuable benefit."

For organizations looking for extraordinary benefits, Causey says to look at the resources at your disposal to come up with unique ideas that will also be cost effective.

"Look at what is special about your organization and find a way to showcase it," says Causey. "If you are a museum, offer private tours; if you are an educational institution, offer exciting classes. Put yourself in your members' shoes and ask yourself what kind of benefits you would want."

Source: Mackenzie Causey, Membership Manager, The Women's Museum, Dallas, TX. Phone (214) 915-0884. Website: www.thewomensmuseum.org

20. Give Members Royal Treatment

Looking for a way to make members feel special? Invite members to spend a morning with membership leaders.

Have the member join in activities at membership headquarters or have leaders join the member at his/her workplace.

Members will appreciate the attention, your leaders will have a newfound empathy for individual members, and you will identify new ideas for member benefits.

22. Buddies Mentor New Members

The Meeting Professionals International-Wisconsin Chapter (Madison, WI), has developed a mentoring program designed to create teams that will initiate new members to their program.

"The goal of the mentor program is to ensure all chapter members receive the support and professional guidance they require," says Susan Kainz, vice president of membership. "There is a wealth of experience and knowledge in our chapter and there is no greater satisfaction than being able share it with other meeting professionals."

The 370-member chapter enlisted members who have expertise as meeting professionals to support new members on a one-on-one basis. At the January 2009 chapter meeting, 30 new members and buddies were partnered, says Kainz.

When new persons join, the membership committee sends someone to welcome them to the organization. New members are asked if they would like a buddy to help them stay informed about the organization, stay connected with other members, share rides or sit with at meetings.

The buddy mentoring system can also lead to assisting the new member with preparing for the Certified Meeting Professional test.

Kainz offers three tips to successfully matching new members with buddies:

1. **Location:** Chapter members who live in the same city can share rides to member events and connect to utilize professional resources.

2. **Years of experience:** They seek to match members based on years of experience, realizing that a new member who has many years of experience in the industry has different needs than someone just entering the profession.

3. **Students:** These new members are paired with experienced members who have gone through the hospitality programs and the three technical schools in Wisconsin. Members guide students on how to prepare for a career in the meeting planning industry.

Source: Susan Kainz, Vice President of Membership for Meeting Professionals International-Wisconsin and Director of Sales and Marketing of The Delafield Hotel, Madison, WI. Phone (608) 204-9816. E-mail: susank@thedelafieldhotel.com

21. Establish and Offer Reciprocal Membership Perks

People who join your organization expect certain benefits for their dues. Give them even more — and increase the actual and perceived value of their memberships — by partnering with other member-based organizations to offer reciprocal memberships.

Choosing to partner with organizations that typically generate high traffic — such as museums, zoos, theaters, country clubs and landmarks — offers extra value and may also bring new traffic to you.

Need more incentive to seek out and partner with other member-based organizations? Know that reciprocal memberships:

✓ **Help encourage renewals.** When members can visit attractions in other cities for free or at a discount, they know they can save money while traveling for business or recreation.

✓ **Provide convenience and familiarity.** Golf enthusiasts and other sports club members enjoy the ability to charge fees, accommodations and meals to their home accounts when entertaining friends or clients while out of town. Members who travel frequently may visit reciprocal facilities more often than they are able to visit yours, valuing being welcomed at both sites.

✓ **Can boost premium membership sales.** Most supporters may want only basic memberships that include discounted admissions, your newsletter and gift shop discounts, but a membership with reciprocal privileges stretches much further for those who take advantage of it. While a basic membership may be $50 per year, a premium membership can still be a bargain at $200.

✓ **Bring new faces to your facility.** Members of other organizations using their reciprocal memberships with your organization may bring persons with them, which can lead to those persons becoming members.

✓ **Boost networking opportunities.** Through reciprocal memberships, you will be in contact with counterparts in other cities who likely are looking for professional connections. Building relationships and affiliations with other prestigious institutions adds cachet to your own. New prospects who review your partnerships and alliances will see they are in good company by signing on with you.

23. Affinity Program Caters to 50-plus Crowd

Being aware of changing needs within your community can lead to new membership options.

Staff at Wesley Medical Center (Wichita, KS) created the group, Wesley Friends, after recognizing a need for programs that promote wellness among older persons. For persons 50 and older, the group emphasizes the importance of healthy living and staying active. Members enjoy discounts, as well as social and educational opportunities.

"We saw there was nothing offered in our community for this age group to help promote a healthy lifestyle and aging well," says DeAnn Most, manager of senior services. "We wanted something that was deemed exclusive for this age group."

Since its inception 14 years ago, Wesley Friends has grown to 7,700 members. Annual dues are $15 per person or $25 per couple.

Most says they look to continually increase the value of membership through new benefits, such as VIP status while in the hospital; discounts at area merchants; dental, vision and hearing plans; health screenings; and travel opportunities.

Source: DeAnn Most, Manager of Senior Services, Wesley Medical Center, Wichita, KS. Phone (316) 962-8400. E-mail: wmdc.wesleyfriends@hcahealthcare.com

---

Create Age-specific Affinity Programs

DeAnn Most, manager of senior services, Wesley Medical Center (Wichita, KS), offers tips to create affinity programs for particular populations:

- Have leadership with a vision and passion;
- Build strong relationships with community partners;
- Create a well-rounded program, even if it means thinking outside the box;
- Ask for help when needed;
- Develop a strong support system from a sponsoring company.

---

24. Offer Members the Chance to Be Mentored by Other Members

If you're looking to boost your membership base, consider beginning a mentoring program for new members.

A well-executed mentoring program can ensure the success of new members and bring them to a new and more committed level of membership. In addition, the program can draw attention to your membership organization, which can lead to new members.

Follow these seven steps to mentoring program success:

1. **Develop mentoring materials to ensure success of the new program.** If your organization does not already have a handbook, create one that is specialized to ensure the success of the mentoring program. Detail program requirements, goals and provide contact information for new members.

2. **Mentor trainings.** Develop a training schedule incorporating mentor training and continuing education for ongoing success of the program.

3. **Develop a schedule for implementation of the new mentoring program.** Determine your organization's goals for the new mentoring program and develop a checklist with outlined steps of accomplishment for the mentor and the new members to accomplish over a set course of time. Design milestones that the new member and the mentor can accomplish together.

4. **Assign partners.** Pair experienced members with new members to introduce the new members to the traditions and expectations of the membership organization. Consider assigning two or three new members to experienced members who are willing to take on the challenge of mentoring more than one new member.

5. **Implement steps to take** in the event a mentor/new member pairing is not suitable.

6. **Design recognition and awards** for mentoring accomplishments and for new members' completion of their checklists to reinforce the program.

7. **Evaluate the new program within six months of implementation.** Design feedback forms that will be completed by mentors and new members to determine the effectiveness of your new program.

Qualities of Ideal Mentor Leaders:

- ✓ Well-regarded within the organization.
- ✓ Exhibit a positive outlook on the membership organization.
- ✓ Strong leadership skills.
- ✓ Able and willing to devote two to three hours per week mentoring.
- ✓ Willingness to work one on one with new members.

---

25. Publicize You Members Through Your Website

Seeking a creative, non-traditional benefit for your membership? Offer a link to member websites from your organization's website.

The Kansas Auctioneers Association, Inc. (KAA) of Newton, KS and the Citizens for the Arts in Pennsylvania (Harrisburg, PA) offer this benefit. It was a marketing decision for both.

LaDonna Schoen, executive director, KAA, says members have been taking advantage of this benefit for the past nine years. "The KAA's decision was a public relations move to better inform the public about the advantage of hiring professionals in our field."

One hundred fifteen members utilize the option. "The cross linking of the websites attracts a greater number of clients to our site. The more avenues to reach potential clients, the stronger the association becomes and the more our members benefit from the increased publicity," says Schoen.

Jenny Hershour, managing director, Citizens for the Arts in Pennsylvania, says "Member organizations should market members and that's why we have offered this feature on our website over the past 14 years. We thought our visitors should be able to click on our members' hyperlinks and go directly to their website."

Almost three-fourths of the organization's 300 members take advantage of the benefit.

To view KAA's website, visit: www.kansasauctioneers.com/members/sites.php. For the Citizens for the Arts in Pennsylvania, visit: www.citizensfortheartsinpa.org

Source: LaDonna Schoen, Executive Director, Kansas Auctioneers Association, Inc. (KAA), Newton, KS. Phone (316) 283-7780. E-mail: kaaauct@cox.net
Jenny L. Hershour, Managing Director, Citizens for the Arts in Pennsylvania, Harrisburg, PA. Phone (717) 234-0959. E-mail: jlh@citizensfortheartsinpa.org

26. Host Free Family Fun Days to Boost Interest

To give your organization community exposure, host regular free events for families.

The Sonoma County Museum (Santa Rosa, CA) hosts a Free Family Day on a Saturday every other month, says Patricia Watts, chief curator. Workshops offered for children and adults relate to the main gallery exhibition, boosting visibility of the latest exhibit as well.

On Free Family Day, the museum is open 11 a.m. to 5 p.m., with workshops usually starting at 1 p.m. and running throughout the afternoon.

Patricia Watts, chief curator, cites tips that make the organization's free days a success, and which can be tailored for your family-friendly member event:

- **Getting the word out.** Having a full room of participants is what makes the event a success, Watts says. Send the news to members and nonmembers. Staff send weekly e-mails to museum members detailing free day information, inform the local newspaper, list the event on invitations for museum exhibitions to 2,000 homes and place flyers at the museum entrance.

- **Offering a crowd-pleasing artist or workshop.** Hosting an appropriate artist or workshop is important to drawing people to the event, Watts says. Consider what age group the artist works best for and focus on attracting that age group to the event. The museum staff receives positive feedback from persons who take part in

workshops in which they are able to complete projects and take them home.

- **Stocking up on supplies.** Having enough supplies for the event also is important. "If people have signed up and you run out of materials, having disappointed participants is not good public relations," Watts says.

- **Limiting participant numbers.** Watts says to keep the event organized and be sure plenty of supplies are available, the museum staff require workshop participants to make a reservation. Typically, 20 to 50 participants are accepted.

- **Securing donations.** The museum solicits donations from local businesses to pay for the activity materials. Donors are attracted to sponsor the event with such benefits as having their business logos on the event flyers. Signage also is included at the event to thank donors.

- **Seeking feedback.** The staff surveys participants after each event on what they liked and disliked.

Watts says museum staff plan to expand the free family days to once a month.

Source: Patricia Watts, Chief Curator, Sonoma County Museum, Santa Rosa, CA. Phone (707) 579-1500. E-mail: pwatts@sonomacountymuseum.org

27. Include Membership Lectures in Your Benefits Package

The "Member Lecture Series" is an excellent strategy for attracting new members and a memorable benefit for your entire membership.

The Philadelphia Museum of Art (Philadelphia, PA), for example, uses member lectures to bring recent members into the museum soon after they join. According to Membership Director Mark Mills, "Lectures take place at least quarterly, so all new members are invited within the first few months of their membership year."

The membership program manager works with staff and curators to plan new lectures six to 12 months in advance. Because of a dynamic exhibition schedule, lecture topics remain fresh and current. Senior museum personnel serve as speakers. Lectures are promoted through mailed invitation postcards and also through the membership calendar of events. Members are asked to reserve their seats by phone or in writing.

Lectures are typically held at the museum on Saturday mornings and run about one and a half hours long. The lecture series is free to all members.

Space is rarely an issue. Only a portion of the museum's membership is likely to attend a specific lecture. When the lecture is overbooked, the museum schedules a second session on another date or holds both lectures in succession.

Printing and mailing the invitation postcards is the primary expense of the lectures. "Our combined cost for three events over the past year was $3,300," stated Mills. "Given that we had around 12,000 new members during this period, it was quite affordable."

By hosting lectures at your own facility, while producing all materials and invitations in-house, you can slash expenses.

Source: Mark Mills, Director of Membership, Philadelphia Museum of Art, Philadelphia, PA. Phone (215) 684-7852. E-mail: mmills@philamuseum.org

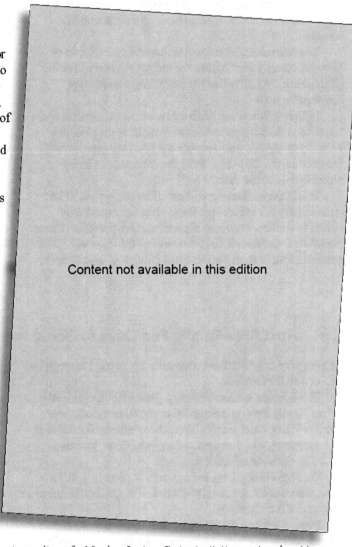

Content not available in this edition

A sampling of a Member Lecture Series invitation postcard sent to new Philadelphia Museum of Art members.

28. Expand Online Member Benefits

How often do you evaluate the member benefits you offer?

Increasing numbers of organizations are offering online member perks as part of their total benefits program. Here's a small sampling of online benefits to consider:

✓ **Screensavers** — Provide access to several different screensavers with images related to your organization's mission and programs.

✓ **Education, training, certification opportunities** — Make e-learning available.

✓ **Online store** — Offer gift items at a member discount that can only be purchased online.

✓ **Audio features** — Give members-only audio tours or special podcasts of interest.

✓ **Access to online publications** — Provide members exclusive insider news and opinions.

✓ **Links to members' sites** — Allow website visitors to connect to members' professional or personal websites.

✓ **Networking** — Allow members to network with one another via a member directory, bulletin boards, listservs, chatrooms and more.

✓ **Job opportunities** — Provide members the opportunity to list job openings and search job openings via your website.

29. Keep Members Engaged With Premier Membership

Offer a premier membership with exclusive benefits to attract new participants.

The Cultural Center at Ponte Vedra Beach (FL) offers the Renaissance Society as its premier membership level.

"This is a wonderful group of community leaders who support the arts," says Sandy Argroves Wilson, director of development and marketing. "We developed some exclusive benefits to keep this group engaged."

Those benefits include:

✓ Private parties in homes of other Renaissance Society members.

✓ Access to exhibiting artists during a private opening reception.

✓ Discount on art sales at exhibition openings for top-level members.

✓ Early invitations for events.

✓ Discounts and receptions at Cultural Center partner establishments.

"They have so much fun that members often invite their friends to join without prompting from staff," she says.

Formed in 2007, the society has 100 charter members and is fast moving toward a goal of 300 members.

Source: Sandy Argroves Wilson, Director of Development and Marketing, The Cultural Center at Ponte Vedra Beach, Ponte Vedra Beach, FL. Phone (904) 280-0614. E-mail: sawilson@ccpvb.org

30. Member Discounts? Endless Possibilities

What discounted products or services are you currently offering your members? Depending on the type of organization you represent, there's no end to what you can offer (assuming your costs are minimal).

Consider these and other member discount possibilities:

- ❑ Insurance
- ❑ Services you offer
- ❑ Car rental rates
- ❑ Name brand products
- ❑ Airfare rates
- ❑ Entertainment
- ❑ Sports
- ❑ Lodging
- ❑ Dining
- ❑ Computers
- ❑ Career, job services
- ❑ Advertising rates
- ❑ Educational offerings
- ❑ Conference fees
- ❑ Shopping discounts
- ❑ Phone rates
- ❑ Travel tours
- ❑ Books, gift items
- ❑ Pick up, delivery services
- ❑ Printing, copies
- ❑ Internet access

31. Offer Members Ball Games, Treasure Hunts and More

Host a treasure hunt as a fun and memorable way to get members together.

At The Florida Luxury Marketing Council (Coral Gables, FL), a treasure hunt "is always a hit because it's a great team builder, and it permits everyone to see a part of town they wouldn't otherwise," says Christopher Ramey, council chairman. "Everyone made great memories, and the pictures prove it."

To set up a successful treasure hunt for your members, Ramey says:

1. **Pick treasure spots.** Choose six to nine locations you want teams to find (number depends on amount of time for your event and the distance between spots).

2. **Write clues.** Enlist creative staff or members to write poems that reveal clues directing the teams to each of the different locations.

3. **Arm teams with cameras,** then set them on their way with clues and instructions that the first team back with photos of all the sites wins!

4. **Get ready to celebrate!** Set up refreshments and hors d'oeuvres for all to enjoy at a party at the end of the treasure hunt.

Ramey suggests two more events popular with members:

Dine arounds: Make reservations for area restaurants. Include a variety of eating places. Create a board for members to sign up where they want to eat out together.

Baseball games: "No one minds if you buy the least-expensive tickets, and there is still magic about being in a ball park," he says.

Source: Christopher Ramey, Chairman, The Florida Luxury Marketing Council, Coral Gables, FL. Phone (305) 371-9130. E-mail: cpr@floridaluxurycouncil.com

32. Offer Members a Nanny Option

What is your organization doing to accommodate your members with children? Consider creating a nanny or caregiver option, to make membership more accessible for families.

Christy Novak, membership and event sales manager, Minnesota Children's Museum (St. Paul, MN), says the museum has been offering a nanny option since 1998. For $20 (in addition to the membership fee), families can add a caregiver to their membership.

"The nanny option was created to meet the needs of the working family that has a caregiver for their children. We see a lot sold before summer vacation begins or during other school breaks. It allows parents to send their children to take part in the museum when they are unable to attend themselves," says Novak.

Novak says this person is able to attend the museum with the parents and the child. "Families can add more than one nanny who can be a named person or a rotating caregiver at any point in their membership." Around 10 percent of the museum's members take advantage of the program.

The nanny option is promoted on the museum's website as well as on membership flyers, brochures and newsletters. Families receive two membership cards to share between themselves and the nanny. The cards list the two adults, the number of children and the word "nanny."

"By offering this program we are able to accommodate the needs of the working family who want their caregiver to bring their children here to play and learn," says Novak.

Source: Christy Novak, Membership & Event Sales Manager, Minnesota Children's Museum, St. Paul MN. Phone (651) 225-6010. Website: www.mcm.org

Content not available in this edition

33. Offer Members Free 'Dino-mite' Deals

Free admission to museum exhibits and events brings benefits to members and the organization.

The California of Academy Sciences (San Francisco, CA) is offering its members a "dino-mite" deal with free admission to its popular dinosaur exhibit.

"Members always receive free admission to temporary exhibits; it's a standard members' benefit," says Marilyn Cahill, associate director of membership. "Free admission is a good sales incentive for new membership sales and encourages members to renew. Members, of course, can visit the museum for free every day."

During the exhibit, admission prices are raised for nonmembers. The academy touts this as a good time to renew memberships or become members to enjoy a great

exhibit and additional savings.

Free academy lectures also are offered to members as part of their membership package. About 75 to 80 percent of the audience attending the monthly lectures is academy members. Lectures by academy scientists are the most popular. The academy boasts a total of 93 people, including curators, in its research division.

Members pay admission for the special lectures held at the academy, but they do receive a discount. These special lectures are used as an incentive for new members. If they become a member at the door, they receive free admission.

Source: Marilyn Cahill, Associate Director of Membership, California Academy of Sciences, San Francisco, CA. Phone (415) 321-94103. E-mail: mcahill@calacademy.org

34. Allow Members to Join Your Speaker's Bureau

Allowing members to become part of your speaker's bureau will increase exposure for them and your organization while adding another membership perk.

Any member can fill out a request form and join the speaker's bureau of the Greater New Haven Chamber of Commerce (New Haven, CT), says Janet Testa, vice president, operations.

The online application asks for complete contact information, whether the member has presented before, a list of topics and any special equipment required. Information is uploaded to the chamber's website where any visitor can review it, learn about the speakers and make direct contact with them, if desired.

"This takes us out of the loop and gives the parties a chance to decide if the fit is good," says Testa.

She adds that placing the information in a public online venue means no worries about recommending certain members over others. "We do not represent any proficiency or make a recommendation," she says. "Everything is done directly between the parties."

An added bonus? The online feature drives more traffic to the chamber website.

Currently, 75 members belong to the speaker's bureau. The chamber lists speaker's bureau topics in nine categories: Financial information; sexual harassment in the workplace; career development; leadership; healthcare; tax strategies; marketing; current issues and security.

The online speaker's bureau "is a great advantage of membership," Testa says. "We can offer members an opportunity to appear before an audience as an expert in their field, which we hope will translate into business for them."

Source: Janet A. Testa, Vice President, Operations, Greater New Haven Chamber of Commerce, New Haven, CT.
Phone (203) 782-4323. E-mail: Janet.Testa@gnhcc.com

35. Insurance as a Member Service: the Benefits and Liabilities

Since first offering term life insurance in 1985, the Penn State Alumni Association (University Park, PA) has come to offer every type of personal coverage except pet insurance, jokes Patrick Scholl, director of business and finance at the association.

Scholl shares some of the insights he has gained over years of offering insurance to the largest dues-paying organization in the country.

Why offer insurance as a service to members?

"For one, we receive revenue from the underwriters — not a commission on individual policies, but a guaranteed yearly amount. The program has become our third-largest source of income. Just as important, though, we feel we offer a valuable service by sifting through the numerous providers and plans out there so we can say to members, 'This company is reputable. We stand by them.'"

Should organizations look for a program administrator first, or start with an underwriter?

"I would recommend starting with the administrator because those that have good reputations will bring top-rated providers to the table.

"Administrators are very important. They should be able to put together a complete marketing plan — brochures, solicitation letters, ads in alumni magazines — and then execute that plan. But they should also provide back room support. If a member has a claim rejected, you want an ad-ministrator who will be a strong advocate with the insurance company."

How involved is your association in the day-to-day details of the program?

"We supply our administrator with mailing lists and review and approve promotional material, but beyond that we are not directly involved in promoting or marketing of the insurance products. The actual mechanics of processing claims is similarly handled by the underwriting companies — Liberty Mutual, John Hancock, New York Life.

What types of insurance would be good places to start?

"Auto/home and life insurance are consistently among our most widely used products. Short term medical (six months or less) has also been popular with graduating students."

Are there downsides to offering insurance?

"Some alumni might object to receiving what they see as junk mail from the association. Also, people who have bad experiences with their policy often attribute that situation directly to the association itself. Because the promotional mailings all carry your organization's name and logo, you really have to be serious and do your homework before offering anything in the marketplace."

Source: Patrick J. Scholl, Director of Business and Finance, Penn State Alumni Association, University Park, PA.
Phone (814) 863-2809. E-mail: pscholl@psu.edu

36. Extend Benefits for Members in Financial Need

During these tough economic times, some membership organizations may experience a lower-than-normal renewal rate. If you find member numbers dropping off because of economic hardship, take steps to inspire them to rejoin when their economic status takes a turn for the better.

Membership staff with the Milwaukee Art Museum (Milwaukee, WI) got creative when they began getting calls from members saying they were not renewing their membership because of job loss. During a fall 2008 team meeting, staff decided to extend membership for these members, at no charge, for four months.

"We are hoping that this gesture will earn us much good will when these former members do find employment later on," says Sara Stum, director of membership.

The four-month extension is only offered to members who contact the museum's staff regarding their inability to renew specifically because of job loss. Since the museum uses bulk printing and mailing rates, Stum says, the cost of these membership extensions is considered minimal.

She says they plan to continue the effort as long as the unemployment rate remains above normal.

"Members have been very grateful and surprised" with the four-month extension, says Stum. "We hope that they repeat this to their friends and keep us on the top of their lists of places to continue to support when their circumstances improve."

If your organization cannot afford to extend benefits at all membership levels, consider extending modified benefits to members in need. For example, consider including certain basic benefits and services, such as newsletter mailings, but excluding more costly services. Members will appreciate the effort and hopefully rejoin your organization when they are able.

Source: Sara Stum, Director of Membership, Milwaukee Art Museum, Milwaukee, WI. Phone (414) 224-3248. E-mail: Sara.Stum@mam.org

37. Help Your Members Network More Successfully

Many members attend meetings and other special events for one reason: to network.

But while the thought of networking may be what brings them to the event, "most members never take advantage of the opportunities to make real connections with others," says Thom Singer (Austin, TX), an expert in social networking and developing a personal brand. "Since all opportunities come from people," Singer says, failing to connect with others at membership events "is a waste of time and money."

As a membership director, look for ways to help your members network with one another — and to gain that important benefit from your organization. Singer offers five ideas for doing so:

1. **Say the word, networking, often.** Remind members at networking events, such as lunches and happy hours, that now is a good time to meet new people. Go beyond simply hosting an event, and put networking on the top of their minds.

2. **Give them tools to connect.** Offer networking games at conferences or meetings. If your event has booths, encourage members to visit each one to be eligible for a prize. Post "secret shoppers" in the crowd to give out $5 gift certificates to those who are networking well. Have members go in search of the person holding "the golden business card." It is fun, and allows them to meet a lot of people and ask meaningful questions to learn about each other.

3. **Encourage friend-making.** Discourage people from sitting with the members they already know. If five people from one company sit together at a table, they will not meet anyone new.

4. **Boost online interaction.** Via your organization's website, establish a "mini online social network." This will allow conference attendees to log into this when they return home. They can share with other members what they have learned at the conference, and have discussions with each other on an ongoing basis about specific topics.

5. **Gently pull people out of their comfort zones.** Membership directors and conference organizers need to discourage cliques. Make sure speakers, panelists, board members and other VIPs are approachable and involved with the crowd.

Singer developed The Networking Quiz, an interactive survey that helps professionals measure and compare networking skills. Take the quiz at www.networkingquotient.com.

Source: Thom Singer, Author/Speaker, Austin, TX. Phone (512) 970-0398. E-mail: thom@thomsinger.com. Website: www.thomsinger.com

38. Weekend Trips Strengthen Museum Membership

The more ways you can connect members with one another through positive special events and opportunities, the better they will feel about choosing to belong to your organization.

One member benefit growing in popularity is a travel club or trip component of membership. For example, staff at the Hunter Museum of American Art (Chattanooga, TN) connect members by offering unique weekend trips to nearby destinations. By selecting trips that offer art appreciation opportunities, participating members can enjoy what bonds them together — art.

In addition to enjoying art offerings at the destination, members also explore and enjoy the locale's shopping, dining and entertainment venues as well.

The museum's latest trip to Savannah, GA, gave members a weekend taste of a location six hours from Chattanooga. Couples were able to participate in the trip for $590 and singles for $295. Staff were also offered the trip at a discount to encourage their participation.

Eileen Henry-Haun, development associate and volunteer coordinator, offers the following tips for planning a member travel trip:

❑ Publicize the trip in all member communications to include the member newsletter or magazine, website and send e-mail blasts.

❑ Open the trip to nonmembers. The Hunter Museum of American Art advertises trips to nonmembers at a higher cost to include the cost of membership. This way a new member is signed on to the organization and enjoys the trip as a member.

❑ Plan trips on a regular, set timeline. The Hunter Museum of American Art offers trips in the spring and fall each year so members can plan ahead for each getaway.

❑ When possible, connect the trip with what is currently offered at your organization. A recent trip for Hunter Museum of American Art members included a tour of a historic home in Savannah, GA, similar to the museum's 1904 Southern Colonial building. The reciprocal program that the Hunter Museum of American Art takes part in allows members to go to many other museums for free.

❑ Tap hotels at the destination for information on local restaurants, shopping destinations and other sightseeing venues that may interest your trip guests. Ask for unique stops to avoid tourist traps.

❑ Prepare an itinerary for the trip that details times when members will come together for meals or other activities but also allows for free time where guests can venture out on their own. Include details as to what is covered in the cost of the trip so members know what meals are included within the price of the trip.

❑ Check with the local chamber of commerce for more tips and suggestions about the area you're visiting. Ask the chamber to provide maps of the city to give to your members.

❑ Design an affordable trip for members. Add all the expenses to be sure the price of the trip includes those costs and allows for a cushion to accommodate unexpected expenses.

❑ Offer a discount to staff to encourage their attendance on the trip and to foster camaraderie between staff and members.

Source: Eileen Henry-Haun, Development Associate and Volunteer Coordinator, Hunter Museum of American Art, Chattanooga, TN. Phone (423) 267-0968. E-mail: ehenryhaun@huntermuseum.org

39. Discount Sales Thank Members, Increase Revenue

Offering members a special discount to shop in your store can result in increased sales and serve as a way to show your gratitude to your members.

Members of the Ann Arbor Hands-On Museum (Ann Arbor, MI) regularly receive offers of 10 percent discounts in the museum's store and enjoy a special four-day double discount sale in early December, which features a 20 percent discount on everything in the store.

"Our member double discount days are offered to reinforce the importance of members to our organization," says Mel Drumm, executive director. "'Double' implies an extra value; it encourages members to shop in our store for their holiday gifts and increases museum traffic. It also provides a value-added exclusive benefit that saves members

money. In addition, it is a small thank you for their continued support."

They promote the sale through e-mail blasts to some 4,000 members, the newsletter that is mailed to members, on the museum's website and by posting announcements in the store.

Tracking member purchases during the annual discount sale shows an increase of up to 40 percent in purchases, Drumm says: "We have some members who wait for the sale to get holiday shopping done; we do it early enough to accommodate Hanukkah shoppers. We have even gotten one or two new memberships out of it."

Source: Mel Drumm, Executive Director, Ann Arbor Hands-On Museum, Ann Arbor, MI. Phone (734) 995-5439.

40. Member Loyalty Cards Create Incentive to Join, Get Involved

Since Jan. 1, 2009, members of the Kirkwood-Des Peres Area Chamber of Commerce (Kirkwood, MO) have earned Chamber Rewards points by attending meetings, paying dues on time, advertising in the chamber newsletter and taking part in other activities.

Points are tracked with the personalized barcode member card system, Scan Me In, (St. Louis, MO) developed by Marilyn Elkin, The Barcode Lady LLC (St. Louis, MO).

Members earning the minimum required points are entered into a monthly drawing where they're eligible to receive one of three prizes valued at $25 or more. At month's end, the total points return to zero so every member begins the new month at the same level. However, total cumulative points are recorded, allowing members the opportunity to win quarterly prizes and one big annual prize.

Chamber staff record member points simply by scanning a member's card with a handheld scanner, then upload scanned information onto the office computer with specialized software that tallies the points earned.

"By introducing the Chamber Rewards cards, our underlying goal is to increase member retention," says Gina March, vice president of marketing for the chamber. "More importantly, this is a fantastic benefit to our members at no cost."

The card (shown below) boasts the logo of two major sponsors of the new rewards program — the sponsor who purchased the cards on behalf of the chamber; and the sponsor donating the first annual grand prize of a furnace and installation ($2,300 value).

The card can also be used to provide member-to-member discounts at member businesses and discounts at participating restaurants. March says both of these added-value benefits work toward the chamber's goal of having members bring at least 5 percent of their purchasing back to the community.

The program has been easy to implement, March says: "It's the easiest thing to get sponsors for the prizes because they get to draw the name of the winners and award the prizes themselves. It's all about giving members exposure."

March also created a prize catalog to coincide with the rewards program, offering another outlet for members to advertise their businesses.

Sources: Marilyn Elkin, The Barcode Lady LLC, St. Louis, MO. Phone (314) 821-1400.
E-mail: MidwestMarking@earthlink.net
Gina March, Vice President of Marketing, Kirkwood-Des Peres Area Chamber of Commerce, Kirkwood, MO.
Phone (314) 821-4161. E-mail: gina@thechamber.us

Content not available in this edition

41. New Benefits Can Lead to Growth

Offering new member benefits sets the stage for fresh growth in an organization.

The La Crosse Community Theatre (LCT) began new patron benefits for its 2006-2007 season. The offerings offset the downside of success, including turning away would-be theatergoers because season ticket holders take up most of the seats.

The organization has been around for 43 years and has consistently had a large, loyal base of season ticket holders and donors. "Approximately 65 to 70 percent of our seating capacity is season ticket holders," says Sandi Ceason Weber, business manager. "Most community theaters can't even dream of that number."

Now LCT is focusing on the future with new staff, including a director of philanthropy. The organization is also looking for a new, larger theater to accommodate more members. It's the perfect time for LCT to start pushing for growth with new member benefits.

New benefits include:

- **Patron Pick:** Give the audience what they want. A survey gives patrons a chance to say what they would like to see on stage. LCT hopes it's an incentive for new people to join as well.

- **Patron Gala:** Show appreciation to patrons with an invitation-only social event. Plans include a recap performance of the past season with drinks and hors d'oeuvres.

- **Bring-a-Friend Card:** Reward patrons for their generosity and support. They receive a card allowing them to bring two guests to a performance. "We're confident that many people who are introduced to LCT by friends are going to want to come back again," Ceason Weber says.

Source: Sandi Ceason Weber, Business Manager, La Crosse Community Theatre, La Crosse, WI. Phone (608) 784-9292. E-mail: SCWeber@lacrossecommunitytheatre.org

42. Offer Your Members Dream-come-true Trip Opportunities

Fulfill your members' dreams through special events.

The Los Angeles-based American Sailing Association (ASA) offers members a week of sailing in a tropical locale, says Charlie Nobles, executive director. "We wanted to add an event that fulfilled the dream of most of those who had just learned to sail and let them know that our organization truly represented sailing, not just certifications."

ASA administers education standards and certifications throughout the United States for persons learning to sail. Previously, members received basic benefits, including two free sailing magazines and discount coupons.

"The (week-long sailing) event has become a major hit with our existing members, attracts new members to our organization each year and generates a great deal of publicity for us," Nobles says. "Attendance has grown every year."

A key to the event's success is the high level of service to members, he says. This includes personally welcoming each guest; having a personalized gift bag in their hotel room when they arrive; and arranging special activities, even for small groups.

"As a result, the next year, the guests come back and bring more friends," he says. "That is the kind of involvement and response that really builds branding."

"It is much more than just a sailing trip," Nobles says. For $1,195, ASA members receive a week at a resort hotel, meals, free sailing instruction, boats, prizes, gift bags and special ASA parties and events.

Source: Charlie Nobles, Executive Director, American Sailing Association, Los Angeles, CA. Phone (310) 822-7171. E-mail: cn@american-sailing.com

43. Rewards Benefit Eco-conscious Members

If part of your organization's goal is to improve the environment or you simply wish to add a going-green feather to your organization's cap, take a tip from the Albany Pine Bush Discovery Center (Albany, NY).

Prime parking spots at the center are reserved for visitors driving low-emission vehicles and those who are carpooling or vanpooling.

You may also consider placing reminders in your printed and electronic newsletters to encourage more people to receive your publications online, reducing the cost and waste of paper copies.

By implementing these benefits, you can reward those who stay true to your mission and help you reach your goals while increasing your organization's environmentally conscious profile.

44. Consider 'Leave Options' As Member Benefits

Give members more freedom with an option to put their membership on hold.

The La Crosse Area Family YMCA (La Crosse, WI) gives members age 65 and older the option to have "senior leave," says Nate Hundt, membership and marketing director.

"We offer a senior membership with the option to put a membership on hold, because we feel seniors are a specialized population," Hundt says, adding, "Many seniors live on a fixed income and/or often are not around for a period of time throughout the year."

YMCA staff also use this leave option as a recruitment tool.

"Seniors see this option as additional freedom in the membership," Hundt says. "They feel they're receiving a great benefit. They can be gone for three months and not have to pay membership dues or repay the joining fee."

The YMCA puts firm restrictions on the option. While the senior leave option can be used any time of year, it can only be used for three months each year.

"We limit the time frame to provide consistency and limit those individuals that put their membership on hold," Hundt says.

There is no cost difference for those taking the leave option. The monthly senior membership cost is the same, whether or not the member uses senior leave. Those who take advantage of the leave option do save three months' worth of membership dues.

Hundt says the leave option does have its challenges, such as creating additional paperwork and updating computerized membership information.

Another challenge is explaining to persons who request a longer or shorter leave option that it is only available for the three-month term: "In this situation, we have to call or speak with them in person regarding the reason for their three-month leave request," Hundt says. "We tell them that anything less does not qualify and anything longer would require repayment of the joining fee."

Source: Nate Hundt, Membership and Marketing Director, La Crosse Area Family YMCA, La Crosse, WI. Phone (608) 782-9622. E-mail: nhundt@laxymca.org

45. Partnerships Strengthen Memberships

Officials with the Ottawa Valley Tourist Association (OVTA) of Pembroke, Ontario, Canada, created a unique and cost-saving member benefit by developing significant partnerships that enable members to advertise at a lower rate.

Through this benefit:

✓ The OVTA offers its members cost-effective and valuable cooperative advertising that they would normally not be able to afford on their own. The OVTA purchases blocks of advertising space in various advertising mediums, including print, radio and television and sells the space back to the membership at a reduced rate. With this approach, all OVTA members are marketed together providing a stronger advertising impact about OVTA's destination and they're saving 20 to 60 percent off standard ad rates.

✓ OVTA partners with various websites, newspapers and radio stations to offer prizes (provided by members) for contests or promotions in exchange for editorial, on-air time or exposure online.

✓ Members of the OVTA are also invited to participate at the various trade shows in the booth or can opt to have brochures distributed there for a nominal fee.

✓ Every OVTA member has access to the membership list, which can be utilized for networking or communication opportunities.

Building Advertising Partnerships That Are Right for Your Members

Nicole Wilson, communications coordinator, Ottawa Valley Tourist Association (Pembroke, Ontario, Canada), offers three tips for building advertising partnerships that are right for your members:

1. Cater to what your membership wants or needs. Find specific avenues for partnerships that are significant to your members.

2. Work with advertising medium to make the most of financial contributions. For example, don't be afraid to ask for free editorial space to accompany an ad.

3. Measure your results to make sure you are getting the ultimate return on your investment.

By building advertising partnerships for your members, you can assist them in strengthening their businesses and create a bond between members.

Source: Nicole Wilson, Communications Coordinator, Ottawa Valley Tourist Association, Pembroke, Ontario, Canada. Phone (800) 757-6580. E-mail: NWilson@countyofrenfrew.on.ca

46. Sweeten the Pot With Member Benefits

Freebies can be the shiny penny that turns people's heads toward your organization and entices them to want to learn more.

While advertisers have long known that people like to get more than they paid for, increasing numbers of member organizations are capitalizing on the universal desire by offering special benefits to first-time members.

"They are an enticement, but they also answer a question," says Kristin Gregory, executive director of the Carbondale (IL) Chamber of Commerce, of the complimentary benefits her organization has long provided to new members. "They are a tangible answer to the question of how the chamber serves its members in practical ways."

The chamber's benefits to new members (see box to the right) provide something for everyone, but give particular attention to the needs of new or newly relocated business owners, says Gregory. Advertising services, free business consultations and discounted members services are consistently popular with new members, but chamber officials are always seeking new ideas from both current members and members of the chamber's board of directors.

Though membership incentives are directed primarily toward recruiting new members, current members benefit from these incentives, too. By donating benefits — most of the chamber's incentives are provided by current members — businesses raise awareness of their services and make positive connections with professionals who may become clients.

While few, if any, members join the chamber expressly to take advantage of first-time benefits, the incentives do help attract potential members and encourage them to sign on, says Gregory. "They are a bonus that adds value in members' minds, and for that we're glad to offer them. It's just another way to show that we're doing whatever we can for members."

Source: Kristin Gregory, Executive Director, Carbondale Chamber of Commerce, Carbondale, IL. Phone (618) 549-2146. E-mail: kristingregory@gmail.com

New Member Benefits Offered By Carbondale (IL) Chamber of Commerce

- ❑ $100 free advertising in The Southern Illinoisan with purchase of $100
- ❑ Free commercial production with placement of advertising schedule on WPSD-TV
- ❑ 25 percent off purchase of advertising from one of the Wither's Radio stations
- ❑ Free business consultation with Feirich/Mager/Green/Ryan Law Firm
- ❑ 30 minutes free business counseling by Gilbert, Huffman, Prosser, Hewson & Barke
- ❑ Free mailbox for one year at Mail Boxes Etc.
- ❑ $0 down, $39.99 dues at Gold's Gym
- ❑ Buy one get one half price Annual Banquet Tickets (Limit one)
- ❑ One free insert in "The Communicator"
- ❑ One free Monthly Member Luncheon Ticket
- ❑ One free member list or mailing labels

47. Promote Member Businesses With Website of the Month Feature

Visit the website for the South Wayne County Regional Chamber (Taylor, MI) and you'll notice a feature that highlights an individual member's website.

Chamber staff select one member's website to feature on the chamber homepage each month, says Sandy Mull, vice president. Doing so, she says, both encourages members to create a website that promotes their business and brings them more attention.

Chamber staffers rate member sites on appearance, user-friendliness and if a site entices a visitor to want to go beyond the homepage. Mull recommends having clear rules for the selection process so that members who are not selected do not feel slighted.

The chamber also allows members to nominate sites they feel are worthy of attention. Members can even nominate their own sites, but a member website can only be featured once every 12 months.

"We're always looking for services we can provide for our members," says Mull. "'Website of the Month' is just one more way to promote our member's businesses."

Source: Sandy Mull, Vice President, South Wayne County Regional Chamber, Taylor, MI. Phone (734) 284-6000. E-mail: Sandy@swcrc.com. Website: www.swcrc.com

48. Create Members-only Yearbook

A member yearbook is a fun way to share information and get to know one another.

To create yours — either in place of or in addition to an annual member directory — refer to high school yearbooks for layout and category ideas. List members by the year they joined your organization. Include headshots or ask members to submit a photo to include in the yearbook.

Under their photos, list business and family information along with fun facts (e.g., favorite color, favorite subject in high school, favorite author or quote).

Fill other pages with photos and anecdotes from member events, plus member committee highlights and a staff section.

Save printing costs by creating an electronic yearbook to e-mail to members and post on a members-only website area.

49. Make Your Space A Member Benefit

In weighing various benefits you might offer members, give thought to offering available space at your facility that members might book for personal events — anniversary receptions, family reunions and more.

You could make the space free for those who give at the highest levels and at a discounted price for those giving at lower levels. You might even make the space available to nonmembers for a higher fee, with members having first priority.

Remember, anything you can do to encourage people to visit your facilities makes them more aware of your mission and services.

50. Microgrants Support Member Ambitions

At the Northfield Union of Youth (Northfield, MN) nearly 900 young persons make up the membership base. To encourage the entrepreneurial spirit of these members, the Northfield Union of Youth has implemented a program designed to provide funding for members under the age of 19 who would like to begin their own business.

Another local organization — Northfield Healthy Community Initiative — dedicated $5,500 to form the new microgrant program designed to fund the business startups. Student members of the Northfield Union of Youth first submit an application for grant allotments in $1,000 increments. In 2010, members can apply for the grants three times throughout the year.

To obtain a microgrant, student members are required to complete an application. Once the application is approved, the member is then partnered with a business mentor who will help them develop a business plan, complete a second application and guide them in starting their businesses.

Once grants are dispersed, members attend seminars that offer relevant information about starting a business and guide them in developing important business skills.

If your membership is comprised of business-minded individuals, consider implementing a microgrant program that will aid the ambitions of your members.

Amy Merritt, director of the Northfield Union of Youth, shares three ways they help members maximize microgrants:

✓ Assisting them in choosing a product or service that will be exciting and fun to develop.

✓ Asking microgrant recipients to think carefully about who their customers will be. This helps guide them in their advertising and business plan.

✓ Suggesting that members contact staff at the organization to brainstorm business ideas, get help with the application process and find a mentor for their new business.

Source: Amy Merritt, Director of Northfield Union of Youth, Northfield, MN. Phone (507) 663-0715.
E-mail: northfieldunionofyouth@gmail.com.
Website: www.unionofyouth.org

Event Showcases Member Talent

Here's another idea from the Northfield Union of Youth (NuY), Northfield, MN, that showcases member talents: Ask them to incorporate gift certificates featuring their talents in gift baskets for auction.

NuY members created a February 2010 event to support the organization's goals called "I Heart NuY Fundraiser."

The membership of 900 young people banded together to create a Valentine-themed event complete with dance party, photo booth, cotton candy sales and more.

A key element of the festivities was an auction of donated gift baskets that showcased member talents. For example, gift baskets could include dance lessons, bead making lessons or home-cooked meals.

51. Allow Members to Showcase Their Photography Skills

Put your amateur photographers to work with a members-only photography contest.

Whether you are looking for photos to include on your website, membership brochure, newsletter, calendar or other piece, invite members to submit images.

Emphasize that anyone with a digital camera can give it a try. Establish parameters as to what types of images are acceptable, including size and color preferences.

Let members know what the images will be used for and the time period in which you will be accepting submissions.

Include model releases for images that include people.

If you have a large membership base or receive a large number of entries, choose a handful of exceptional images and ask members to vote on their favorite. Make the voting process anonymous and do not list which members took which photos.

Members will enjoy flexing their creative muscles while providing your organization with a wealth of images from which to choose.

52. Create Contests Your Members Will Clamor For

Offer your members the opportunity to win prizes and perks with true value as a major benefit and a perfect way to thank them for their support.

One organization that does so successfully is Imagine It! The Children's Museum of Atlanta (Atlanta, GA). Staff offer members the chance to win special parking privileges for a month at one of two spots in the employee parking lot designated for just that purpose, says Laura Halad, membership coordinator.

"With the average parking lot downtown costing $10 — some days it can be as high as $30 if there is an event — we feel this is a great extra perk," Halad says. "Some of our winners use the spot two to three times a week, some use it once a month, but it is available all month long to the winners."

To enter for the chance to win the parking spot, members fill out a form on the membership table at the museum and place it in an entry box. Members can enter once per visit. The form asks for member name, address, e-mail and car information, as well as the last five digits of his/her membership number.

"I have someone on staff pull the two names the morning of the first of the month and then call the winning families usually between 9 and 10 a.m.," says Halad. "We then mail them a form for their windshield. We require that the winner display a form in their window, to distinguish that they are permitted to park in our employee lot."

To let members know about this perk, she says, "We mention it to members in several ways. We have it on a rotating basis in our monthly e-newsletter, and we also mention it when guests join the museum at the front desk. In addition, our security desk is next to the membership table and they mention it to guests as they come onto the museum floor."

This simple yet worthwhile membership benefit, created by the museum's former director of marketing more than three years ago, is a favorite among members and staff, Halad says.

Content not available in this edition

"Members love it, and our staff use it when they talk about memberships and the perks we have," she says. "Some months I have 100 entries and some months I have 10. It depends on traffic and word of mouth in the museum."

The contest costs virtually nothing as the museum already leases a parking lot for employees and guests of the museum on official business such as board meetings, interviews or meetings with development and other departments, Halad notes.

For organizations without access to a private parking lot, she advises purchasing a parking spot in a public lot as a contest prize, or providing one-time preferred parking for a special event.

Source: Laura Halad, Membership Coordinator, Imagine It! The Children's Museum of Atlanta, Atlanta, GA. Phone (404) 527-5910. E-mail: laura.halad@imagineit-cma.org

53. Appreciation Month Celebrates Members

Show your members how much you value their support with an entire month dedicated to thanking them.

Membership staff at The Children's Museum of Richmond began offering a member appreciation month in April 2005. The first celebration marked the museum's fifth year in a new building, says Stacy Smith, membership coordinator.

Since then, the annual event has grown in ways it honors members as well as in its ability to raise awareness of the museum in the region.

"We started member appreciation month as a way to show our members how much we appreciate their support and how much they mean to The Children's Museum," says Smith. "They are an essential part of our museum, and we want to show them how important they are to us."

The month-long celebration has included a raffle with prizes, such as a special delivery of cupcakes by the museum's mascot, Seymour, and an art studio visit for a small group of children.

In addition, members may bring a guest for free every day during member appreciation month, a benefit that has been very well received by members, Smith says.

Organizers are looking to further enhance the special month.

"Instead of the raffle, we are focusing on all of our members by adding more performances and activities that will happen during the appreciation month, such as our 'Member Monday' evening program," says Smith. "This event is like a mixer where members come and socialize. It is publicized on our website and by invitation. We usually have child-friendly food, such as chicken fingers, fruit, veggies, etc. It is always held at the museum since this is an opportunity for our members to have the museum to themselves."

Cost for the special evening gathering for members varies, she says, noting that the 2007 event cost under $400.

What type of incentives you are able to offer members throughout an extended celebration will depend on what size

A member button (below) featuring the logo (right) of Children's Museum of Richmond (Richmond, VA) lets members share their support throughout the community.

Content not available in this edition

budget your organization has. If your budget is limited, Smith suggests that offering discounts on items/ programs may be more cost effective than hosting events.

Also, consider starting off with a member appreciation weekend or week if you are not sure a membership month would be feasible.

Smith says she and her co-workers ensure all members are aware of the celebration so they can take full advantage of the programs and activities that have been planned for them. "We publicize our member appreciation month on our website, our membership brochures and mailings, and at the museum with banners and posters."

A member appreciation month is a fun way to thank your members and remind them how much you value their contributions, she adds.

"Our members have enjoyed the additional activities and events we provide for them during this month and consider it an added benefit of their membership."

Source: Stacy Smith, Membership Coordinator, The Children's Museum of Richmond, Richmond, VA. Phone (804) 474-7011. E-mail: ssmith@c-mor.org

54. Include Member Milestones On Your Event Calendar

If your organization has an online event calendar, consider including member celebrations such as birthdays and notable anniversaries along with special event listings.

Each January, send out a mass e-mail to membership asking them to let you know of important milestones coming up that year, such as a retirement, 25th or 50th wedding anniversary, etc.

Including these special dates on your online calendar helps staff keep track of and acknowledge them while en-

couraging members to send good wishes as well.

In addition to including dates on your calendar, include a congratulatory message on your website addressed to the member celebrating a special occasion.

While some members may not wish to have their birthdays or other events listed, many members may appreciate the recognition. What's more, it serves as a free and relatively easy way for you to connect with your members.

55. Offer Financial Aid To Members in Need

Offering financial assistance with memberships can help attract members who may not otherwise be able to participate in your organization.

The La Crosse Area Family YMCA (La Crosse, WI) offers qualifying members a financial assistance program. Currently, about 20 percent of members receive aid, says Nate Hundt, membership and marketing director.

Offering financial aid is an important part of the YMCA's mission as a community-based organization, Hundt says. "Financial assistance allows everyone of all abilities and ages the chance to participate in our programs," he says.

Financial assistance funds are provided to members through YMCA's annual Strong Kids Campaign, the United Way and La Crosse Community Foundation. To be eligible for a scholarship, a member must fill out a form requesting financial assistance and provide proof of income.

The YMCA provides a quick response to these applications. Those who turn in their completed applications by Friday are notified the following week on Wednesday. Once they receive notification of their acceptance, they need to activate their membership within two weeks.

"The YMCA welcomes people regardless of their ability to pay," Hundt says. "Our programs are designed for people of all ages, abilities, faiths, ethnic groups and incomes."

Source: Nate Hundt, Membership and Marketing Director, La Crosse Area Family YMCA, La Crosse, WI. Phone (608) 782-9622. E-mail: nhundt@laxymca.org

56. Cater Services to Seniors

Do your services embrace special needs and preferences of your older members?

The mission of SeniorNet (Santa Clara, CA) is to provide persons age 50 and over with education and access to computer technologies in an effort to enhance their lives and share their knowledge with others.

SeniorNet began in 1986 and boasts a membership of 15,000. Most members and volunteers are age 50 and above.

Executive Director Kristin Fabos, who has substantive experience working with an aging membership, offers advice to meet older members' needs:

✓ **Realize communication is critical to members over age 50.** Those trained at SeniorNet's learning centers are comfortable with online communications. Gauge the technology knowledge of seniors in your organization to determine the best mode of communication (e.g., direct mail rather than e-mail). The key element is to communicate with senior members on a consistent basis.

✓ **Encourage community-building activities.** Feeling a sense of belonging is important to seniors. Offer these members reasons to gather (e.g., member potluck, monthly birthday get-together) and ensure other members their age will attend.

✓ **Offer senior members leadership opportunities.** Allowing seniors to take part in the organization by heading up a function or organizing a member event gives them a sense of importance and their passion and level of commitment will only benefit your organization.

✓ **Seek out advice and comments from senior members.** Those over age 50 offer a wealth of life and professional experience. Tap into that to better your organization.

Source: Kristin Fabos, Executive Director, SeniorNet, Santa Clara, CA. Phone (408) 615-0699 or (800) 747-6848. E-mail: kfabos@hq.seniornet.org

57. Give Student Members Exceptional Benefits at Reduced Cost

The Society for Nonprofit Organizations (SNPO) of Canton, MI, offers a student membership at a discounted rate for college students embarking on a career in the nonprofit sector.

Professors familiar with SNPO who have students going into the nonprofit field alert them of this opportunity. Some require use of the membership in course curriculum.

"Our student membership can be a good replacement for a traditional course pack and offers students access to nonprofit information contained at our website," says Jason Chmura, membership director. "We hope that students going into the nonprofit sector will carry their student membership into their careers and become lifelong members."

Student members can purchase individual memberships at $29 per year giving them access to current articles, ar-

chived materials and other relevant nonprofit materials.

Chmura shares three ways student memberships strengthen a membership base:

1. Student memberships encourage becoming a member for those who might not consider membership on their own at the normal rate.

2. Student memberships introduce new individuals to your brand who likely don't already have preconceptions or other biases.

3. Offering student memberships builds good will toward your organization.

Source: Jason Chmura, Membership Director, Society for Nonprofit Organizations, Canton, MI. Phone (734) 451-3582. E-mail: jchmura@snpo.org

58. Membership Travel Clubs Offer Your Members the World

Have you considered a travel program that allows your members to travel the world?

The University of Oregon Alumni Association (Eugene, OR) has included a travel program component for nearly two decades. Members can take part in trips offered through travel company partners to destinations such as Greece, China and Antarctica.

Trip participants are usually a combination of alumni from various universities, according to Lauren Peters, assistant director for membership. "Because of the nature of these trips, the high quality, timing and pricing," Peters adds, "the demographic tends to be our more mature alumni."

Ranging from one to two weeks and costing $1,600 to $3,200 per person, the trips draw an average of 150 members a year.

Itineraries are featured on the association's website (www.uoalumni.com/travel).

If 20 or more association travelers take part in a trip, the travel company offers a complimentary trip that is used by a staff member or past board president, who acts as trip host.

Peters say they currently work with two travel companies: Thomas P. Gohagan & Company (Chicago, IL) and AHI International (Rosemont, IL). When choosing destinations, she says, they consider the success of past trips, informal feedback from members interested in certain destinations and travel history of other alumni associations.

If planning to create a travel program, Peters says, "realize that most travelers are older; they have the time and money, so look for trips that would be comfortable for them. Then throw in some trips that are a little more adventurous for younger members. Start slowly — with fewer trips — to see what works and what doesn't, and build from there."

Source: Lauren Peters, Assistant Director for Membership, University of Oregon Alumni Association, Eugene, OR. Phone (800) 245-2586.

Content not available in this edition

Stunning online brochures help spread the word among current and potential members about travel opportunities available through the University of Oregon Alumni Association.

Encourage New Members With 'Top 10 Reasons to Join' List

Travel to exotic locales with fellow alumni is just one perk offered by the University of Oregon Alumni Association (UOAA) of Eugene, OR. Other perks, cited in the online list, "Ten Reasons Why a UOAA Membership is Valuable," include:

✓ Dues fund programming that connects alumni, students, friends, and UO faculty to build a stronger university and UO pride.

✓ Career networking and mentoring opportunities through online services and career-focused events.

✓ Online and print communications that update and connect alumni to the university and one another.

✓ Invitations and discounts to UOAA events and services.

✓ Support of legislative and congressional advocacy efforts to increase state and federal support for the university.

✓ Student scholarships through the UOAA-endowed $250,000 scholarship fund.

✓ Football tickets, UO gear discounts and tax deduction on 80 percent of dues.

View the list in its entirety at: www.uoalumni.com/s/1202/index.aspx?sid=1202&gid=1&pgid=409

59. Gear Programs to Member Life Stages

Understand the generational and career stages to more efficiently attract and retain members.

There are three distinct career stages encompassing various generations in the business environment, says David Nour, managing partner, The Nour Group Inc. (Atlanta, GA).

"Understand each stage and align where your membership is," Nour says.

Nour explains the three stages and their significance:

Stage One — Growth and Scale: These are younger members (Gen X, Gen Y or Millennium) climbing the steep corporate, social and economic ladder. Many are single or have young families. Create community and family-oriented programs and opportunities for these members to engage these other valuable aspects of their lives.

Stage Two — Significance: These are Baby Boomers and Early Matures with solid careers still climbing the ladder but not as steep. Their primary focus is still on the social and economic ladder but they're also interested in balancing their lives. They also have older children so they're more open and more involved in events or programs on a regional or national level.

Stage Three — Legacy: These are Matures and those near or at retirement. Work is optional and they're focused on philanthropy and leaving a legacy. Many have grandchildren and are looking for interesting experiences. They would make great possible mentors, board members or advisors.

Go for diversity in your organization. "Recruit a diverse, broad-based membership from each of the generations and professional stages," Nour says. "Beyond physical diversity, most of us understand and aim to attract diverse mind sets, perspectives and abilities to execute the organization's mission and goals."

Source: David Nour, Managing Partner, The Nour Group Inc., Atlanta, GA. Phone (888) 339-1333. E-mail: dnour@nourgroup.com

60. Member One-day Sale Has Many Benefits

Everybody loves a bargain! Use this fact to offer a unique perk to your members and raise the interest of potential members.

For instance, if your organization has a gift shop or an online store, offer a half-price event for members. You could choose a handful of items to mark 50 percent off for one day only, or perhaps offer a smaller discount on a larger number of items.

Turn your sale into a recruiting effort by requiring each member to bring a nonmember to your physical site or invite one nonmember to the sale in your online store in order to receive their discount. Each nonmember who is brought in by your current members can be added to your mailing list for future campaigns.

In addition, consider offering a discounted membership fee, or other incentive, for all those who sign up on the day of the sale.

Offering members a one-day sale is a great way to encourage them to purchase your logo merchandise, helping you to get the name of your organization out in your community and making room for new items in your store.

61. Added Benefits Can Boost Member Renewals

Looking for a way to sweeten the pot for renewing members? Try setting up a multi-tiered program with added benefits for each additional year of membership.

You can let members know about the added benefits up front or at renewal. Informing them up front allows them to see that benefits will grow over time, along with their membership.

You can even offer an incentive to encourage members to pay for a multi-year membership. Letting them know at the time of renewal gives them incentive to renew and adds value to the membership.

62. Give Members a Reason to Belong

Persons looking for motivation to join the Mooresville-South Iredell Chamber of Commerce (Mooresville, NC) don't have to look far. The chamber's website posts 10 reasons why membership with the chamber is so important:

1. **New business contacts.** Networking and new business contacts help your business grow. With nearly 1,100 members representing thousands of area employees, the chamber speaks with a strong voice for our business community.
2. **Credibility.** Credibility to make a statement that you are committed to the future of Iredell County.
3. **Leadership development.** Learning opportunities/professional development to help you run a smarter, more profitable business.
4. **Community commitment.** Promote the community to help residents enjoy greater opportunities.
5. **Referrals.** Referrals and sales opportunities to deliver return on your investment.
6. **Publicity and exposure.** Publicity and heightened name recognition so customers know who you are.
7. **Marketing and advertising.** Targeted and affordable advertising to help your business effectively grow on any budget.
8. **A healthy local environment.** Create a strong local economy to keep our business momentum moving forward.
9. **Gain a voice in the government.** The chamber is your representative on the local, regional, state and national level. Your voice is heard on vital regulatory, legislative and educational issues affecting your business.
10. **Activities.** Getting involved in the many activities the chamber has to offer leads to valuable relationships and gratification in serving the community.

Source: Karen Shore, President/CEO, Mooresville-South Iredell North Carolina Chamber of Commerce, Mooresville, NC. Phone (704) 664-3898. E-mail: kas@mooresvillenc.org

63. Thank Members With VIP Programs

Looking for a way to thank certain members for their participation and support? Consider creating a VIP program that provides a select group of members with additional benefits and services.

In February 2008, staff with the Lake Champlain Regional Chamber of Commerce (Burlington, VT) created a VIP program for members who frequently attended their business after-hours networking events.

"We wanted to do something that thanked our regular business after hours attendees and highlighted them to the other members," says Susan B. Fayette, director of member development & benefits.

The VIP program application asks for a $45 one-time fee, basic contact information, credit card information to process the $45 fee to cover program costs and also if the applicant would like a coupon book at a discounted price.

VIP program recipients receive:

✓ A permanent nametag with chamber lanyard to wear at all events which lists member's name, company name and year the company joined the chamber.

✓ A $10 discount on the chamber's $60 coupon books.

✓ Walk-in price of $8 per event ticket, a $4 savings per ticket.

✓ Entry in a monthly drawing featuring sponsor-donated prizes such as restaurant gift certificates.

✓ Advance notice regarding special events.

✓ An invitation to the chamber's annual VIP-only luncheon, which is paid for by a sponsor and is free to attend.

✓ Placement of the VIP member's name and company listed on the VIP page of the chamber's website.

✓ Special check-in at events, which includes the member's nametag waiting for them at the check-in table as soon as they arrive, regardless of whether they have pre-registered.

As of May 2009, some 20 members had signed on for the VIP program. Fayette says members often ask how they can become part of the VIP program when they see their fellow members receiving the VIP treatment at events. For the most part, the program has become invitation only, with Fayette reaching out to members at the business after hours events to let them know how they can join the program.

Source: Susan B. Fayette, Director of Member Development & Benefits, Lake Champlain Regional Chamber of Commerce, Burlington, VT. Phone (802) 863-3489, ext. 211. E-mail: susanb@vermont.org

64. 'Content to Go' Provides Members Instantaneous Information

The American Society for Training & Development (ASTD) of Alexandria, VA, has a new benefit for its 43,000 members: Content to Go, an online location dedicated to current information and immediate access to resources in the learning field.

"We started Content to Go a few months ago to provide members with a quick, one-stop place to access content on the learning and development field's hottest topics," says Jennifer Homer, vice president of communications and member relations. "Currently, there are four topics on the page with links to five articles or resources for each one. The topics will continue to grow."

Homer says they chose to create the information-packed database to centralize the organization's many resources.

"ASTD has a great deal of content available (to members) on our website in different formats: magazine articles, podcasts, research reports, e-newsletters, webcasts and more; we created the Content to Go benefit to pull together content on hot topics in the learning field and make it available to members in one convenient place."

Source: Jennifer Homer, Vice President-Communications and Member Relations, American Society for Training & Development, Alexandria, VA. Phone (703) 683-8100. E-mail: jhomer@astd.org

---

Offer Your Members 'Content to Go'

Interested in offering an online resource that consolidates important member information in one location? Jennifer Homer, vice president of communications and member relations for the American Society for Training & Development (ASTD), offers these tips:

1. Use survey results to determine the most relevant topics in your members' industry or field.

2. Provide content in different formats; go beyond print-based articles and include resources like podcasts, webcasts and videos.

3. Regularly update content and communicate to members when new information is available.

---

65. Family Days Attract New Memberships

Looking for a new way to reach potential members? Consider offering family days to promote your membership.

The University of Texas (UT) Club (Austin, TX) hosts family promotions, a program that offers members, spouses, children and members' guests the opportunity to partake in family activities monthly.

"We want to grow children as 'little club members,' while entertaining the parents and providing a great family atmosphere that feels like a 'fun' club," says Jenny Campbell, membership director.

"This has been a great strategy for recruiting potential new members."

To promote the family activities, the UT Club distributes a newsletter to more than 3,800 members, sending weekly mailers and e-mail blasts, and posting signs and flyers throughout the club.

Some of the family promotions include:

Kid Movie Nights — Children watch a movie, have snacks and play games in a separate room while parents have private time to enjoy a gourmet dinner at reduced prices.

Weekend Winery Tours — Members take a motorcoach tour of local wineries. It's a great excursion for couples, seniors or older children.

Family Baseball Outings — Participants enjoy a local, minor league baseball game on a party porch. Games, typically held on Friday nights, end with a fireworks show.

Friday Night Football Rallies — Cheerleaders from the University of Texas perform to tunes by the alumni band. The mascots pose with families for pictures and a gourmet buffet dinner is served.

Campbell says some events range from $15 to $40 per member (kids are free). Events such as the happy hours and pep rallies are free.

"The key to our success is that we try really hard to create a professional and fun family atmosphere," says Campbell. "We truly think it's this unique, private club setting with a mix of creative events that warms up to members."

Source: Jenny Campbell, The University of Texas Club, Membership Director, Austin, TX. Phone (512) 477-5800. E-mail: contactus@utclub.com

66. Recruitment Rewards Stimulate Membership Growth

To recruit members, some organizations offer enticing rewards. For ultimate results, consider bestowing incentives on both the newcomers and those who recruit them.

The National Association of Counties (NACo), Washington, D.C., has successfully provided recruitment incentives for nine years. Current NACo members who recruit new member counties, as well as the newly recruited county, both receive a free conference registration valued at $690 to use at one of three conferences.

"Albeit an expensive reward, we have shown that it pays off in immediate engagement and return attendees," and pays for itself in return attendance by the new members, says Andrew Goldschmidt, director, membership marketing. "It is a win-win for all, including recruiters, new members and conferences."

Incentive Brings in 15 to 20 Members a Year

NACo officials promote the incentive through its state associations, direct mail, e-newsletters and e-mail signature messages (see box).

"We receive 15 to 20 of our members (about 10 to 20 percent) from this program each year," says Goldschmidt.

NACo staff use contact management software to track members' recruitment efforts, he says. "Our (Avectra) database has an integrated contact management software module that is one of the vital tools of our efforts. We have notes about 'who recruited whom in there so we credit it when it comes in per the notes."

In most cases, the member who did the recruiting notifies the organization, says Goldschmidt. "We get both types of notifications, but a little heavier on the sponsor (current member) letting us know. Sometimes the new members say 'I joined because of Jake at Otero County, CO, etc.' It is about 70 percent sponsor notifications and 30 percent new member notifications."

NACo staff honor the year's top recruiter with a feature story in a member publication and a trophy at the board of directors meeting at its annual conference. Runners-up for top recruiter receive a gift such as a bottle of wine or specialty item.

Providing Incentives Takes Planning, Budgeting

To be able to give the free registrations as part of the membership incentive, says Goldsmith, "I have to budget for the conference registration charge backs in one line item and the trophy/other awards in another." He says $300 is the true hard cost of the registration while $690 is the list price. Costs for the ceremony total another $300.

Goldschmidt says they surveyed members about incentives and found the free registration "as the only one that would really be 'attention getting.'"

Linking Members, Mentors

The recruitment incentive does more than just boost membership numbers, says Goldschmidt; it helps engage recruiters and helps new members attach to mentors, which helps with new member retention (the most precarious renewal segment): "By giving both the recruiter and new member one free registration, we are taking a risk, but our retention rate is at a record high of 98 percent (including new member counties), so it is an investment now, that pays off and then some in the long run."

Source: Andrew S. Goldschmidt, Director, Membership Marketing, National Association of Counties, Washington, D.C. Phone (202) 942-4221.

"It's a win-win for all, including recruiters, new members and conferences."

Sponsor a New Member Program

Attention officials from members of NACo

Receive a free conference registration if you sponsor a new member county, parish or borough. Here is how it works:

1. Notify the NACo membership department who you are sponsoring by calling 202-393-NACo.
2. Indicate whether you would like NACo to send membership information on your behalf or if you would like materials on membership to send on your own.
3. When the county, parish or borough joins NACo, the NACo membership department will contact you to award you your registration.

It's that easy! Start recruiting now and you and the new member benefit (they also get one free conference registration for joining).

Contact Andrew Goldschmidt or Emily Landsman for more information.

---

67. Personalize Member Gifts, Incentives, Rewards

Member organizations give out renewal rewards, anniversary gifts or other perks to their members. If you do so, consider personalizing gifts based on member suggestions.

Include a question on member applications and member surveys that asks them to list specific gifts or rewards that they would like to receive (see sample, right).

Make it clear that you are just asking for suggestions so that your members do not feel disappointed if they suggest "jewelry store gift certificate" and do not receive one. For example, state: "We are looking for suggestions to reward you, our all-important members, for your loyalty. Please share your three favorite ideas for gifts that you as a member would enjoy receiving."

Ask them to be specific. For example, say: "Please name the establishments from which you would like to receive a gift certificate."

Record answers in a database to which you can refer when deciding on gifts or rewards to give members.

The responses will help you better serve your members while providing insight into their likes and dislikes.

How Can We Say 'Thanks'?

At XYZ Organization, we're constantly looking for ways we can better serve you, our valuable members. To help us in that area, we'd like your input on possible ways we can say thanks.

Your name: _____

Your e-mail: _____

Please check any/all items that you as a member would enjoy receiving as a thank-you gift:

- ❑ Gift certificate to (be specific): _____
- ❑ One free guitar or singing lesson
- ❑ A free massage at a local salon
- ❑ Free session with dog walker or pet sitter
- ❑ Tickets to a film or comedy show
- ❑ A bottle of your favorite wine
- ❑ Other: _____
- ❑ Other: _____
- ❑ Other: _____

We appreciate your input as we strive to improve our member services. To learn more about membership benefits, please call us at (555) 555-5555 or visit us at (Web address).

Please mail this questionnaire with your membership renewal form or fax to (555) 555-5556. Thank you!

68. Celebrate Members' Birthdays

Celebrating members' birthdays — especially those of children — will serve as a delightful benefit.

At Virginia Living Museum (VLM) of Newport News, VA, parents sign up children, ages 3 to 12, for the birthday club at the admissions desk and online, says Gina Shackelford, membership manager.

"Each month I send out a postcard to all the children with birthdays for that given month. The postcard can be redeemed for a small treat on their next visit," usually a pencil personalized with "Happy Birthday from the VLM" or a themed prize coordinated to the current changing exhibit.

The birthday club, created several years ago, is maintained entirely in-house. Postcards feature a paragraph about options for celebrating birthdays at the museum, along with instructions to bring the card in for the birthday gift.

While Shackelford oversees the data entry, bulk mailings and purchasing supplies, volunteers help label postcards and prepare gifts. Admission desk personnel hand out the gifts and collect the postcards.

Depending on the type of gift bestowed, you may need to create a separate budget to accommodate mailings and gift purchases, she says. She pays about $500 a year for postage and $100 for gifts. For the postcards, she buys cardstock or uses paper left over from special events.

The birthday club, Shackelford says, "is a popular benefit since many members also have their birthday parties here. It has potential for other uses too. For example, the VLM celebrated its 40th anniversary and we invited club members to have cake with us at a special event."

Children's birthday wishes also go out in VLM's quarterly newsletter.

Museum officials promote the birthday club on its website, mention it in all welcome and renewal letters and in the benefit flyer, says Shackelford. She notes that of 1,900 birthday postcards sent in 2006, some 371 were redeemed.

Source: Gina Shackelford, Membership Manager, Virginia Living Museum, Newport News, VA. Phone (757) 595-1900, ext. 240. E-mail: membership@thevlm.org. Website: www.thevlm.org

69. Host Annual Get-togethers Members Can Brag About

Give your members exclusive opportunities they can tell others about, and watch your membership numbers grow.

Members of The Field Museum (Chicago, IL) receive many special privileges, including priority admission to special exhibits; discounts on workshops, field trips and classes; and invitations to members-only events, including Annual Members' Night.

Members have enjoyed the annual event for 58 years, says Michelle Clayton, director of membership. It's a popular behind-the-scenes look at the museum's collections and laboratories. She attributes the event's success to a culmination of many aspects and efforts to improve the event throughout its six-decade history.

Here, Clayton shares tips on making an annual member event more successful:

✓ Host your member event in March or April to avoid competing with summer events.

✓ Piggyback the members' event with another exciting happening at your organization. The Field Museum hosts the annual members' night in conjunction with a springtime exhibition opening, combining marketing efforts for both events.

✓ Use all resources to market your event. Museum staff sends invitations, spotlights the event in the membership magazine and sends e-mail blasts to members and lapsed members. The e-mail gives lapsed members a great reason to rejoin, says Clayton, noting that this year's efforts netted 166 responses from lapsed members, which translates to a net gain of $15,000 in membership dues.

✓ Offer a free pass to members, encouraging them to bring a guest to the event, increasing the opportunity to gain new members the night of the event.

✓ Post knowledgeable staff or volunteers at membership tables or booths at the event to answer questions about your organization and to sign up new members.

Source: Michelle Clayton, Director of Membership, The Field Museum, Chicago, IL. Phone (312) 922-9410. E-mail: mclayton@fieldmuseum.org

Annual Members' Night Is Great for Members and Staff

Offered for nearly six decades, Annual Members' Night at The Field Museum (Chicago, IL) gives members — currently 39,000 strong — behind-the-scenes access to all aspects of the museum.

Michelle Clayton, director of membership, says they have expanded the event from one evening to two evenings to better accommodate members. For the 2009 event, nearly 6,000 members and their guests attended the Thursday night event and 9,000 attended Friday evening.

Members and guests are allowed to go behind the scenes for a personal view of the exhibition design department and exhibitions that have yet to be unveiled to the media. Members are also asked to offer input, by way of a survey, on several topics including voting on titles of future exhibitions.

Staff pull out all the stops for this popular event, Clayton says, offering members the ultimate entertainment experience. This year's event focused on the museum's newest exhibition — Real Pirates — and included historians who volunteered in full pirate regalia, mingling with guests, offering historical information about the exhibition and creating photo opportunities.

Both nights, every department in the museum delivers a presentation or prepares an activity, giving guests a comprehensive experience. For example, in the zoology department, members were allowed to see flesh-eating beetles at work.

Clayton notes that the event is not only valuable for members, it's a perk for staff, as well.

"Our entire staff loves this event," she says. "During the annual members' night, we have 99.9 percent of our staff here, including the president, who attends both nights."

70. 20 Member Benefit Ideas

Are each of the following benefits for your members?

1. Discounts.
2. Mission-specific informational newsletter, magazine and/or journals.
3. Insurance program.
4. Professional development.
5. Legislative advocacy.
6. Affinity programs.
7. Conference registration discount.
8. Expert advice.
9. Networking opportunities.
10. Volunteer opportunities.
11. Print and online membership directory.
12. Mentoring program.
13. Honors and awards.
14. Access to publication archives.
15. Career advancement tools and assistance.
16. Professional Code of Ethics.
17. Reference library.
18. Members-only website content.
19. Invitations to members-only events.
20. Members-only listserv.

71. Reach Out to Employees of Your Corporate Members

If your organization offers corporate memberships, offer additional benefits aimed at the employees of those corporate members to entice them to join your organization.

Membership officials with the New England Wild Flower Society (Framingham, MA) began offering corporate memberships in the fall of 2007.

"Our corporate membership benefits include free passes to our garden for employee and/or customer use," says Karen D. Pierce, director of membership. "The primary reason we offer these free passes is that it is an attractive benefit for our corporate members."

Number of passes offered depends on level of corporate membership: The highest level ($5,000 annually) receives 100 passes. The middle level ($2,500 annually) receives 50 passes and the lower level ($1,000 annually) receives 25 passes. Each pass is good for one regular admission (a value of $8 for adults and $5 for children over age 3).

"We specifically decided to offer one-time-use passes instead of revolving passes or discounted memberships in the hopes that once employees visit our garden, they might want to join on their own, paying full price," says Pierce.

The passes also provide contact information from those who use them.

"Our corporate passes include a statement on the front that says: 'Good for one free admission to Garden in the Woods when information on reverse is provided.' On the reverse, we ask for date of use, company, name, address and e-mail," says Pierce.

They use this information to track visitation for reporting back to the member company and for membership solicitation purposes.

While they have yet to gain members through the free pass benefit, Pierce says they plan to include employees who have used the passes in a future member recruitment campaign. She adds that about 25 percent of the passes offered have been used.

Source: Karen D. Pierce, Director of Membership, New England Wild Flower Society, Framingham, MA. Phone (508) 877-7630, ext. 3801.

Content not available in this edition

The brochure for the New England Wild Flower Society (Framingham, MA) highlights VIP tickets to special events as a benefit of corporate membership (see "Return On Investment," bottom left). The organization also offers free admission passes for corporate members to share with staff.

72. Offer Special Membership For Grandparents, Seniors

The Sedgwick County Zoo (Wichita, KS) offers a unique membership level geared to its aging membership called Grandparents Plus.

Members who are grandparents are offered a wide array of benefits under the program, including the opportunity to bring all their grandchildren to the zoo, no matter the number of children.

"We have a lot of grandparents who are very involved in their grandchildren's lives," says Lynn Duncan, membership manager. "Sometimes the grandparents are more established than the parents and this program allows them to bring all their grandchildren and an additional adult to the zoo."

According to Duncan, this program benefits a broad span of visitors by allowing more flexibility and affordability. For $105 per year, grandparents, grandchildren under 21 and even an adult child of the grandparent all benefit by having the ability to visit the zoo together.

Grandparents are required to be present when using the membership, which Duncan notes helps to foster a true extended family experience. The zoo, in turn, realizes a higher visitor rate.

How did the zoo identify this need? Duncan says longtime members who wanted to remain active at the zoo voiced this need to zoo staff. As a spin-off to the Household Plus program, where nannies can bring children from one household, the zoo then offered the similar plan for grandparents.

The program is well-received, with grandparents enjoying the benefit of bringing their grandchildren any of the 364 days a year the zoo is open, says Duncan — even a member who has 22 grandchildren.

"This is our way to get everyone together at the zoo to foster the zoo as a safe, family-oriented space," the membership manager says of the membership option for grandparents.

Source: Lynn Duncan, Membership Manager, Sedgwick County Zoo, Wichita, KS. Phone (316) 660-9453. E-mail: LDuncan@scz.org

73. Influence Member Renewals

People consider whether to renew memberships year-round, not just when the invoice comes, so be sure each experience they have with your organization is a positive one, says Rhoda Weiss, chair and CEO, Public Relations Society of America (PRSA), New York, NY.

Weiss recommends:

- **Creating a best practices library.** If your association has many chapters, districts, regions and/or special interest sections, share stories online of successful member recruitment or communications programs. Read about what worked and didn't. Share your stories, too.

- **Involving members in recruitment.** In PRSA, local chapters search the media for names of new PR professionals. Invite these newcomers to your organization and ask them for names of co-workers who may be interested in joining your organization. Offer rewards for bringing in the most new members.

- **Giving discounts.** Offer coupons for prospects to attend events at low or no cost, and a lower dues structure initially for new professionals and recent college graduates.

- **Celebrating senior members.** "Tap into their wisdom by asking them to serve in a mentorship group, speak on panels of experienced professionals at a program, facilitate a workshop, judge awards competitions or scholarships and more," Weiss says. "Match their passion to the particular project." And remember that recognition goes a long way.

- **Creating a sense of community** with in-person groups, e-groups, casual gatherings, etc. "No matter the association, members rate networking as one of the most important benefits of organizational meetings," Weiss says.

- **Surfing the Internet** to learn about other organizations' recruitment, retention and promotional activities.

Source: Rhoda Weiss, Chair and CEO, Public Relations Society of America, New York, NY; and President, Rhoda Weiss & Associates, Santa Monica, CA. Phone (310) 393-5183. E-mail: Rhoda.weiss@prsa.org

74. Offer One-of-a-kind Benefits to Top Contributing Members

Have you considered rewarding your highest contributing members with "knock your socks off" benefits?

Here are a few examples of exclusive top-giving-level benefits:

Oklahoma History Center (Oklahoma City, OK):

Special Collector Set of Three Centennial Commemorative Coins. This coin set commemorates the Oklahoma statehood centennial (celebrated in November 2007). Because the coins are limited, Paul Lambert, membership coordinator, says they make a nice premium for the 17 members of the $1,000 Director's Circle and the $5,000 Oklahoma History Center Benefactor levels. The coin set is valued at $185.

Bronze Marquette (6") of H. Holden's "Monarch at Rest." Those members exclusive to the $5,000 Benefactor level receive this reproduction of H. Holden's sculpture of a buffalo at rest that sits in front of the history center. The miniature sculpture is valued at $300.

Cleveland Zoological Society (Cleveland, OH):

Director's Choice Surprise. This could mean attending a zoo baby's birth, participating in on-grounds research or animal relocation. Nine members in the Benefactors' Club ($5,000 to $9,999) and Founders' Club ($10,000 or more) may get to witness these once-in-a-lifetime opportunities.

Veterinarian's Choice. Members of the Benefactors' and Founders' Clubs are invited to witness a scheduled procedure or exam on one of the animals from the zoo's collection at their world-class veterinary facility.

Special Exhibit Sponsor. Donors at the Founders' Club get the opportunity to select a traveling or permanent exhibit to be named after them for one year.

Flamingo Round Up and Release. Beginning at the Directors' Club level ($2,500 to $4,999) and above, donors are invited to participate in releasing the zoo's flamingos in the spring or gathering of the flamingos in the fall for transport to their winter holding. Twenty-two members may take advantage of this benefit.

Source: Paul Lambert, Membership Coordinator, Oklahoma History Center, Oklahoma City, OK. Phone (405) 522-0317.
E-mail: pfl9@cox.net
Tara Turner, Director of External Relations, Cleveland, OH. Phone (216) 635-3323.
E-mail: turner@clevelandzoosociety.org

75. Honor, Retain Members With Emeritus Status

Establish an emeritus category to honor and retain longtime, committed members.

The Cowboy Artists of America (CAA) of Tempe, AZ, offers emeritus status for members who can no longer meet the organization's requirements due to poor health or age-related issues, says Steve Todd, business manager.

This is not a retirement category, Todd notes. Emeritus members continue involvement, but not to the degree of active members. They attend meetings and activities, continue to produce artwork and offer current members the benefit of learning from their experience.

Major CAA membership requirements — a trail ride and participation in an annual art exhibition and sale — require serious commitment that an older member may no longer be up to, Todd says, "It's demanding personally and professionally. Age and health can take its toll. We established the emeritus category for members in good standing, who are not able to fully participate in the show and/or trail ride."

Emeritus members may continue to use the coveted CA (Cowboy Artist) symbol on their artwork, and bring up to two new pieces to the annual exhibition. They are no longer eligible for awards.

Members are voted into CAA, established in 1965, through an intense process of scrutiny by membership. Only CAA artists may use the CA symbol, which sets the standard for Western art throughout the world.

CAA has 23 active members; 12 honorary members who are not artists but significantly contributed to the group; and seven emeritus members who range in age from 77 to 91, says Todd, an honorary member. The emeritus members' photos, bios and samples of work are on CAA's website. Members desiring emeritus status may request it at a formal business meeting. The request must be approved by 75 percent of membership.

"The emeritus members are honored by our group," Todd says. "They had the courage to do this artwork before there was a big demand for it."

Source: Steve Todd, Business Manager, Cowboy Artists of America, Tempe, AZ. Phone (602) 677-3123.
E-mail: info@cowboyartistsofamerica.com

76. Tailgate Contests Equal Fun, Alumni Support

Every college student knows that autumn means football, and football means tailgating.

Now, student alumni associations nationwide are finding that adding a touch of competition to tailgating activities not only provides a great way to connect with alumni, it raises awareness among current students as well.

Here, representatives of three alumni associations that just recently started offering tailgate competitions share details of these member-pleasing events that typically take place in busy, fan-filled parking lots outside the stadium in the hours before the big game:

Eastern Washington University, Cheney, WA
Years hosting: One.
Pre-registration: Online. Registering participants are sent information packets with pompoms, pennants and other spirit materials.
Publicity: Included in all university homecoming materials.
Judges: Three — all alumni.
Grand prize: Barbecue set (tongs, spatula, etc.) engraved with the EWU logo.
Budget: Less than $100.
Unique feature: Improvisation. When only four teams pre-registered, staff of the EWU alumni association took information packets around the stadium parking lot, registering an additional 18 teams (one of which took second place).
Best tip: "Choose judges with great personalities. They can get the crowd going and make sure everyone has a lot of fun."

Pittsburg State University, Pittsburg, KS
Years hosting: Two.
Pre-registration: Telephone. Participants were asked to give the number of a cell phone they would carry the day of the contest.
Publicity: Notice on alumni relations website, blast e-mail to four-state area, press release to local newspaper, reminders in campus newspaper.
Judges: Three — two university advancement staff and one board member.

Grand prize: A pass to private box seating in the university stadium.
Budget: Negligible.
Unique feature: Internal publicity. Contest winners are announced at pre-game pep assembly and pictures are shown on the stadium screen during the game.
Best tip: "Recruit a couple groups already known for tailgating. If one really stellar group signs up, others will follow."

University of Cincinnati, Cincinnati, OH
Years hosting: One.
Pre-registration: None.
Publicity: Notice on alumni association website, e-mail to active area alumni, links in general alumni communications, fliers distributed at previous football games, mention in athletic department communications.
Judges: Three. The development director of the alumni association, one member of the association's student alumni council, one representative of a primary sponsor.
Grand prize: Tailgating package including UC-branded folding chairs, seat cushions, blankets, etc., plus items provided by the major participating sponsor.
Budget: $125.
Unique feature: Local tie-in. Staff at the UC alumni association partnered with two well-known Cincinnati area food producers to host two tailgate cook-off contests — a Gleer's Goetta cook-off and a Skyline Cincinnati chili cook-off.
Best tip: "Leverage a locally known name/product to enhance recognition and interest. Using something novel like a cook-off contest adds value to the game-day experience."

Sources: *Whitney Kiesling, Assistant Director of Alumni and Constituent Relations, Pittsburg State University, Pittsburg, KS. Phone (877) 778-2586. E-mail: wkieslin@pittstate.ed*
Lisa Poplawski, Director of Alumni Advancement, Office of Alumni Advancement, Cheney, WA. Phone (509) 359-4555. E-mail: lpoplawski@ewu.edu.
Keith Stichtenoth, Associate Executive Director, University of Cincinnati Alumni Association, Cincinnati, OH. Phone (513) 556-4344. E-mail: Keith.Stichtenoth@uc.edu

77. Create a Menu of Incentive Possibilities

Granted, the type of incentives you offer potential members depends on the type of organization you represent and the programs and services you provide. Within those parameters, however, there is no limit to membership incentives you might consider.

Why not create a menu of incentive ideas (such as those shown here) from which to choose depending on the type of

promotion and the group you are targeting?

Membership Incentives Possibilities:

❑ Extended (free) membership.
❑ Reduced conference registration.
❑ "Trash and trinkets" — lapel pin, certificate, etc.
❑ Booklet of useful information.

78. Membership Incentives Result in Big Returns

Offering an incentive with a membership purchase is the ideal way to increase membership demand at your nonprofit.

At The Magic House St. Louis Children's Museum (St. Louis, MO), every time a person purchases a gift membership, a new membership or renews an existing membership, the member receives a special child-oriented gift.

Since the onset of the incentive promotion three years ago, The Magic House's membership has continued to grow — even in the face of the pending economic shortfalls in many households, says Vicki Muhs, membership manager.

Since the incentive program began, Muhs says, membership has grown 50 percent to top out at 6,000 members. Of course, not all of that growth can be attributed solely to the incentive program, but the incentive has certainly helped, she says.

Connecting the incentive with a holiday or museum theme, she notes, enables staff to consistently refresh the incentives offered to members. For example, during the holidays, staff and volunteers create 900 baskets filled with holiday toys and merchandise, complete with The Magic House logo.

Muhs says the incentive program works especially well during the holidays when gift giving is in full swing, as those purchasing gift memberships pass the incentive gift on to the recipient of the gift membership — a tangible gift.

Two types of incentive gifts are given based on whether the member is purchasing a basic membership or an upgraded magical membership. This spring, basic membership purchasers received a seed packet and gardening tools, while magical membership purchasers

---

Tie Incentive Gift to Membership Renewal

Since offering an incentive gift with each membership renewal, staff at The Magic House St. Louis Children's Museum (St. Louis, MO) have seen membership grow 50 percent and gift memberships increase by 51 percent.

Vicki Muhs, membership manager, offers tips to implement an incentive program tied to membership:

- Tie the incentive to the current season, exhibit or related theme.
- Promote the incentive to gift memberships heavily during the holidays.

To keep incentive gift cost manageable, Muhs says:

- Contact local attractions or restaurants to include donated admittance or meals with your incentive gifts.
- Try to offset the months with expensive incentives with months of inexpensive or free incentives.

---

received a biodegradable planting bucket adorned with The Magic House logo, seed packet, tools, water bottle and a book about gardening.

The average cost of the incentive gift is $5 with the exception of November and December, when cost may be slightly higher.

"It is a wonder how at the end of the day so many people just want 'stuff,' something tangible to take home," says Muhs. "It may be inexpensive, but if it is something visual, it will always grab the attention of your members. Since we first implemented our incentive program, our gift memberships have increased by 51 percent."

Source: Vicki Muhs, Membership Manager, The Magic House St. Louis Children's Museum, St. Louis, MO. Phone (314) 822-8900. E-mail: Vicki@magichouse.org

79. Online Training Offers Member Benefits

An online training program can provide a valuable benefit for your membership.

The National Glass Association (NGA) in McLean, VA, launched its online training program, MyGlassClass. com, in June 2006. It's designed for flat and auto glass companies as a convenient, affordable and comprehensive resource for improving worker skills, enhancing workplace safety and achieving professional certification, says Deborah Schneider, senior manager of education and training. It's also designed for workers seeking to earn professional certification, improve technical skills and comply with training requirements.

What are the advantages of members taking online

training? It's available 24 hours a day, seven days a week and students can work at their own pace. A computer and Internet access are the only tools needed to work on a course.

The biggest challenge to hosting such a large online training program, Schneider says, is to handle the myriad duties involved in managing the system. To handle this challenge and others, Schneider suggests having support for the program from the top of the organization down. Also, put in place people and technical resources needed to manage the program before it begins.

Source: Deborah Schneider, Senior Manager, Education and Training, National Glass Association, McLean, VA. Phone (703) 442-4890. E-mail: debis@glass.org

80. Offer Members E-cards as Part of Online Services

Looking for new online services to offer members? Consider free e-cards, a member benefit that also helps you share your organization's name with a wider audience.

Members of the Mizzou Alumni Association of the University of Missouri (Columbia, MO) have been sending e-cards from the association's website for nine years.

"Offering e-cards is an easy and fun way to engage alumni and assist them in connecting or reconnecting with friends and classmates," says David Roloff, director, membership and marketing.

Alumni choose from nine e-cards, including happy birthday messages, anniversary congratulations and other sentiments. Members can send an unlimited number of cards at no charge once they log in on the association's website.

An online services vendor, iModules, helped develop and manage the feature.

"We design the card graphics and decide what cards to post," Roloff says. "Since there are so many e-cards out there, we decided just to go with what we felt was best and fit into the module's specs."

He says that while the association does not regularly track numbers of e-cards sent, 2007 statistics show that on average, members send roughly 600 cards a month.

"We occasionally promote the use of the e-cards on our homepage and in our alumni e-newsletter," says Roloff. "When we do that, it drives traffic way up."

By branding the e-cards with your organization's name and logo, you are allowing your members to stay in touch with valued

friends while also supporting your organization, Roloff says. "Development of any e-card should include a way for the recipient to return to the association's website to learn more about the organization and/or to send their own e-card."

Source: David Roloff, Director, Membership and Marketing, Mizzou Alumni Association, University of Missouri, Columbia, MO. Phone (800) 372-6822. Website: www.mizzou.com

The Mizzou Alumni Association (Columbia, MO) features free e-cards alumni can send once logged on to the alumni website.

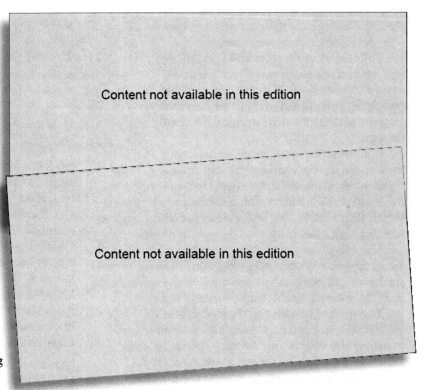

Content not available in this edition

Content not available in this edition

81. Offer Members Travel Discounts

Travel discount benefits are growing in popularity as a member benefit.

Staff with Montrose Travel (Montrose, CA) realized this and developed The MembersOnVacation program.

MembersOnVacation, a free member benefit offered to associations and affinity groups, provides full travel services including airline tickets, car rentals, cruise vacations and hotel reservations to participating associations and their members.

Lisa Fredeen, account executive, says the MembersOnVacation program offers several benefits, such as its revenue share program that gives participating associations and affinity groups a portion of revenue generated by their members' online reservations.

Fredeen says the program is designed to help associations and affinity groups build member loyalty and attract members.

Staff market the program by providing participating associations and affinity groups with a private-label Web link for their website as well as through monthly HTMLs, newsletters and inserts.

Some 50 associations and affinity groups representing 500,000 members offer MembersOnVacation as a benefit.

For more on the MembersOnVacation program, visit www.movaffiliate.com.

Source: Lisa Fredeen, Account Executive, Montrose Travel, Montrose, CA. Phone (818) 553-3215. E-mail: Lisa@montrosetravel.com

82. Strengthen Membership With Reciprocity Agreements

Connect with organizations with similar goals to offer mutual member benefits.

The 350-member Hemet Community Concert Association (Hemet, CA) offers members reciprocity, allowing them to attend concerts of 16 participating associations at no extra charge by simply presenting a membership card.

Diane Mitchell, president, notes that the association, once on shaky ground, has reinforced its strength by banding with other area music associations and offering reciprocity.

Mitchell says the reciprocity program means more members enjoy the talents of area musicians and the musicians have a stronger audience.

To make reciprocity work for your membership, Mitchell recommends:

- Planning car-pooling events. Once a month, offer van service to members to encourage participation at other organizations' events.

- Planning regular e-mail communications to update members on upcoming events or schedule changes of all participating associations within your membership area.

- Making a special effort to announce reciprocal members at each event. Before each concert, Mitchell asks attending members using their reciprocity membership to stand and be recognized.

- Requiring board members to attend events and utilize reciprocity status to remain current on what's being offered within the membership and spread the word about events coming within your association.

- Selecting one point person to create and update the website frequently with new information, consolidate information about the membership and create communications geared to member participation.

- Networking members together before and after events so they can share interests and possibly coordinate rides to upcoming events.

Source: Diane Mitchell, President of Hemet Community Concert Association, Hemet, CA. Phone (951) 927-1775. E-mail: dkmitchell@verizon.net

83. Key Chain Tag Serves as Convenient Benefit Reminder

Many organizations issue membership cards for members to use as identification. Why not issue cards for other purposes?

Since 1996, members of the Newport County Chamber of Commerce (Middletown, RI) have enjoyed a Member-2-Member discount program, taking advantage of available discounts at participating businesses by showing their chamber member key chain tags.

"Once we started the discount program, we quickly realized that there was so much diversity in the types of discounts that we needed a physical thing to give members so that they would take advantage of them," says Jody J. Sullivan, deputy director.

Tags, given free to members, are created by a chamber member who runs a printing business. They are picked up at the chamber office or delivered by staff.

Content not available in this edition

New members receive their discount tag in their welcome packets.

When the program began, members were invited to participate via letter, e-blast and phone calls. Today, new members are asked to participate when they join the chamber. Staff also advertise this program to members and the public as a major component of the chamber's "buy local" campaign.

Currently, 162 chamber members offer discounts to other members through the program.

Chamber staff order thousands of key chain tags annually In fall 2008, for instance, they ordered 10,000 tags at a cost of $2,119.

"Having the physical key tag on your key chain reminds you to use the discounts and keeps the chamber on your mind," says Sullivan. "It also shows the member giving the discount that we are driving business to them."

Versatile key chain tags can also be used in place of traditional membership cards or for benefits such as permanent parking passes for your lifetime members.

Source: Jody J. Sullivan, Deputy Director, Newport County Chamber of Commerce, Middletown, RI. Phone (401) 847-1608. E-mail: jodyjude@newportchamber.com

84. Beyond the Job Bank: Advancing Member's Careers

The online job bank and the career pavilion at the annual meeting are two tried-and-true staples of career advancement benefits available to an organization's members.

But what about complimentary consultations with a dedicated career expert? Or research and networking assistance? Or coaching for when you're considering a career transition?

These are just a few of the many services the American College of Physician Executives (ACPE), Tampa, FL, offers members through its career advancement program.

The ACPE has long made continuing education and career advancement a priority, says Barbara Linney, vice president of career development. Particularly popular among its services are a comprehensive assessment of needs and goals and an interview preparation/practice program. Both services provide structured questions for reflection, an hour-long consultation, and cost $250 for registered members.

Other advancement options include a resume review service, professionally administered diagnostic tools such as the Meyers-Briggs and Disc Inventory assessments, and free "You're Fired – Now What?" coaching sessions.

The ACPE provides a wide range of options, but Linney says most boil down to one simple thing — giving members somebody to talk to regarding their careers.

"Members often just need to talk through where they are on their career path and where they are going," she says. "Training and services are helpful, but simply providing someone who can listen to members is a great place for organization building career services to start."

Source: Barbara Linney, Vice President of Career Development, The American College of Physician Executives, Tampa, FL. Phone (800) 562-8088. E-mail: Blinney@acpe.org.

Career Advancement Options Offered by the ACPE

As a membership benefit, persons who belong to The American College of Physician Executives (Tampa, FL) have access to:

Personal Coaching Services — Private coaching sessions to develop a unique plan and customized instruction for your advancement & success.

Goals & Needs Assessment — $250 members/$450 nonmembers
Work one on one with ACPE's Career Expert to develop a unique outline of your career goals and growth areas.

Interview Preparation — $250 members/$450 nonmembers
Practice the interview session and get useful advice on how to succeed during this critical meeting. Get frequently asked interview questions.

Curriculum Planning — Free to members and nonmembers
ACPE will plan your entire Section 1 schedule as you work towards an MBA or MMM degree or certification as a Physician Executive.

Assessment — Insights into your unique strengths and weaknesses from both a behavioral and performance perspective with feedback from Career Coach.

360 assessment — $500 members/$700 nonmembers

Myers-Briggs — $250 members/$450 nonmembers

Disc Inventory Tool — $250 members/$450 nonmembers

Networking & Research — Background on who and what you need to know to obtain the best position.

Advisor/Mentor — Free to members
We will connect you with an ACPE member who can advise you how to break into the field, how to deal with organizational issues, or give you information about the organization you may be interested in.

Physician Compensation Survey — $150 members/$350 nonmembers
Detailed compensation analysis by position. Used to maximize salary negotiations between you and your employer.

Job Coaching Services — Take everything you've learned and confidently begin your job search following a strategic plan.

Comprehensive Resume — $250 members/$450 nonmembers
A results-oriented resume that will get your resume noticed including a custom cover letter.

Connecting to Recruiters — Free to members
We provide you with a list of reputable recruiters.

Negotiating Contracts & Closing the Deal Video — $55/$75 nonmembers
Video describing what you need to know about yourself to successfully negotiate your next contract, what benefits to expect, and how to not alienate your new employer before you get there — by Sue Cejka.

Career Transition Coaching — How to deal with getting fired & getting over career hurdles.

Trained & Prepared But Getting Nowhere Personal Coaching (30 minutes) — Free to members
You've pushed hard to advance your management education and credentials but you are just not advancing as you had planned. ACPE's career expert will provide tips and strategies for hurdling this apparent brick wall. This complimentary coaching session could result in recommendations for any of the above services or referrals to other resources for support.

85. Member Discounts Prove Popular Incentive

The Washington, D.C.-based American Association for the Advancement of Science (AAAS) offers members several discounts as an added incentive for membership, says Darryl Walter, membership marketing manager.

The association's most popular member discount program is the AAAS/Barnes&Noble.com online bookstore, where members receive an additional five percent off the online price of products purchased.

"The branded bookstore features books reviewed by our publication's book editors on the front page," Walter says. "The store receives a lot of traffic. Barnes & Noble told me recently that we are in their top five business-to-business nonprofit affiliate programs as far as sales."

AAAS officials only choose those discount programs that make sense for their organization and their membership, he says, "They have to have some appeal to our members."

Most companies come to them with discount offers, he says, and since those companies already have discount programs set up, it's usually just a matter of negotiating the discount, evaluating the company and signing an agreement.

Walter suggests that in addition to offering some of the more traditional member benefits such as credit cards and insurance, you also offer some more unique benefits (such as AAAS's Barnes & Noble branded bookstore), as well as those that will have some value to your members.

AAAS partners with a number of other businesses to offer discounts to members, including Office Depot, VIP Transport, Hertz, Geico Auto Insurance, Apple, Seabury & Smith, Portland Press of the United Kingdom, Subaru and subscriptions to The Biochemist.

For specifics, go to www.aaas.org/membership/benefits/.

Source: Darryl Walter, Membership Marketing Manager, American Association for the Advancement of Science, Washington, D.C. Phone (202) 326-6417. E-mail: dwalter@aaas.org

86. Upper-level Membership Perks Encourage Upward Moves

To make your organization's upper-level memberships attract persons of means, provide benefits offering access, recognition or opportunities for socialization, says Lauren Davidson, individual giving manager at the Contemporary Jewish Museum (CJM) of San Francisco, CA.

Davidson explains how her organization incorporates those features into its benefits:

- **Access:** Museum benefits offering access include priority admission, curator-led tours and invitations to exclusive receptions and artist events.

- **Recognition:** Recognition-based benefits include an annual donor wall, newsletter mention and the option to underwrite major exhibitions and programs.

- **Socialization opportunities:** Benefits providing unique opportunities for socialization often focus on travel opportunities such as a tour of a donor's private glass collection or a tour of featured artists' Bay-area studios.

In offering upper-level benefits, museum officials take into consideration that high-end donors may value benefits differently than persons who give at lesser levels. Davidson takes recognition as an example, noting that the desire for public acknowledgement often wanes at the highest giving levels.

"People giving $10,000 to one institution are often giving it to several others," Davidson says, "so recognition is not as important to them. We find (recognition) generally matters more to those in the $1,000 to $5,000 range because many of them give only to us."

Similarly, she says, when offering social opportunities, museum officials often distinguish between on-site events (generally offered at $1,000 level) and off-site events (offered at $1,800 and up), creating a gradation of benefits that encourages individuals to upgrade memberships.

Regarding value benefits such as guest passes and gift shop discounts, Davidson says that when it comes to upper-level donors, "these are not hugely compelling, but they're not meaningless, either," noting that members at the $1,000-plus levels do make use of discounts and special sales.

The most important step to choosing benefits that both reward and encourage members to move up giving levels? Understanding their fundamental motivation, she says: "We find about 75 percent of higher-level donors are mission-based, rather than benefits-based. The key, then, is structuring benefits to make sure those individuals feel involved with the institution they believe in. It all comes back to building and strengthening relationships."

Source: Lauren Davidson, Individual Giving Manager, Contemporary Jewish Museum, San Francisco, CA. Phone (415) 655-7829. E-mail: Ldavidson@thecjm.org

87. E-membership Stretches Membership Base

Membership staff with the American Society for Training & Development (ASTD) of Alexandria, VA, deliver member benefits to their international audience with e-memberships. With dedication to workplace learning and performance professionals, ASTD has stretched its membership to 43,000 by adding an option for members who live abroad.

Jennifer Homer, vice president of communications and member relations, answers questions about e-membership:

How does the e-membership work?

"This is an electronic membership for ASTD members outside of the United States. Members receive all of their benefits electronically."

What are the advantages to e-membership for your organization?

"E-membership is helpful to members outside of the United States. They can access all benefits electronically — research reports, webcasts, T+D magazine, member directory and more (and) reduce their costs by not paying for postage to have the hard copy of T+D magazine mailed to them."

Source: Jennifer Homer, Vice President, Communications and Member Relations, American Society for Training & Development, Alexandria, VA. Phone (703) 683-8100. E-mail: jhomer@astd.org

88. Increase Attendance, Enthusiasm With Rewards Program

To increase member attendance at your special events, create a rewards system to encourage attendance and track participation.

At the Joplin Area Chamber of Commerce (Joplin, MO), the newly created membership program, "FocusOnYou!" (FOY) is an example of such a system that works.

Ginger LaMar, membership director, explains: "Developed as a retention activity program designed to track membership attendance at all chamber activities, the program includes a membership card which enables our members to accumulate points for attendance and volunteerism."

Membership Committee, Chamber come up with concept

LaMar says they implemented the program in January 2006. "Chamber staff and the membership committee researched the concept, developed the product (card with barcode to scan at all events/meetings; electronic scanners; software to capture scans and produce tracking mechanisms), secured underwriters to sponsor cost of materials and prizes and communicated the program's concept and benefits to the membership."

Members accumulate points toward monthly, quarterly and midyear prizes. Prizes include spa packages, appliances, gift certificates and more.

More than 500 members attend program kick off

The program and its custom-designed software were developed in-house to increase membership participation and measure effectiveness of existing programs, says LaMar. More than 500 members attended FOY's official launch.

Costs are covered by the chamber's underwriter sponsor, Joplin Floor Designs, whose logo is also featured prominently on the FOY cards. Cost of printing, mailing and designing cards, plus computer equipment, totals around $12,000.

The FocusOnYou! interactive membership card can be scanned to track individual member attendance at all chamber activities within the Joplin business community. Members also receive scannable key ring tags and cell phone stickers.

"Members can look up points, look up values for events, read information about the prizes offered and compare attendance (point rankings) to that of their peers on the FocusOnYou! website," LaMar says. "The website also lists the prize sponsors and underwriting sponsor."

Members who donate prizes receive recognition based on sponsorship levels. For example, a $500 monthly sponsor will receive logo and prize information in the chamber's monthly newsletter and on its website. Winners and the sponsor companies are mentioned in a weekly e-mail, and a photo of the winner and company owner goes in the monthly newsletter.

The program is increasing awareness and participation, LaMar says. "With higher employee attendance at chamber functions, membership retention went up because employees and employers alike were able to see the benefits of their membership in action. This helped increase member-to-member business, volunteerism by employees and awareness of the community at large, which directly mirrors the chamber's overall mission: 'To improve the economic prosperity and quality of life in the Joplin region, and to be the principal advocate for, and provider of services to, its business community'."

Source: Ginger LaMar, Membership Director, Joplin Area Chamber of Commerce, Joplin, MO. Phone (417) 624-4150. Website: www.joplincc.com

89. In Tough Economy, Be Sure Member Benefits Add Real Value

It's common sense to say your member benefits should add real value. But given the continuing economic slump and high rate of unemployment, communicating this value to your members and potential members is imperative, says Arthur Yann, vice president, public relations, the Public Relations Society of America (PRSA), New York, NY.

PRSA is helping members get the most out of their membership and handle the tough economy with the following efforts:

❏ **Online job center revamp.** A previously static job board was transformed into a popular, interactive resource. They also added a new Ask the Experts feature to complement their Find a Mentor, Content Library, salary information and free résumé posting resources.

❏ **Help with managing budgets.** PRSA is helping people keep their memberships and get more out of them. Recurring special offers include, for example, giving away free chapter or section memberships with the cost of national membership. Members also have the option to pay their membership with quarterly installments. A hardship program to provide assistance with dues for those members who have

been with PRSA for five years or more and find themselves out of work or disabled was also put into place.

❏ **Provision of members-only insurance programs.** Members can now participate in a wide variety of insurance programs, including business and personal insurance, at preferred rates.

❏ **Continuation of free professional development.** Yann says their goal is to hold at least one free webinar per month for members and others in the profession.

❏ **Completion of website overhaul.** New navigation menus and Google-powered search functionality help busy members find relevant information quickly and easily. The new MyPRSA section allows members to create user profiles and contact lists, and indicate preferences that can be used to deliver news and information that appeals to their individual expertise and interests.

Source: Arthur Yann, Vice President, Public Relations, the Public Relations Society of America, New York, NY. Phone (212) 460-1452. E-mail: arthur.yann@prsa.org

Professional Networking Site Links You, Members Online

Could your organization's LinkedIn group be considered a member benefit?

The Public Relations Society of America's (New York, NY) Vice President Arthur Yann, (PRSA), says this online networking connection can certainly benefit members and staff alike.

"We know our members have specific preferences for when and where they consume news and other information about our organization. LinkedIn allows us to communicate with a subset of our members in the way they most prefer, so we know our messages are getting through to them. It also gives us a chance to engage them in beneficial two-way conversations that tell us about their satisfaction levels and other attitudes toward our organization, which we can then collect, analyze and act upon."

Yann says the PRSA gets about 500 requests per month to join their LinkedIn group. Not all of those requests are from PRSA members though, which gives the PRSA an opportunity to encourage them to visit www.prsa.org and learn about some of the other benefits of becoming a PRSA member.

Members have also used LinkedIn to create subgroups that cater to the specific interests and informational needs of their PRSA micro communities, such as districts, chapters and professional interest sections.

90. Appreciation Series Shows Member Benefits

Regular appreciation events can help show members the value of their membership.

This fall the Clay Center (Charleston, WV) started hosting a series of member appreciation events on the second Saturday of every month.

"It's a way to encourage our members to come more frequently and see the value in their membership purchase," says Missy Menefee, membership manager.

A family of four pays $90 for two visits to the museum galleries, planetarium show and giant screen film; a family membership is $75 annually.

To kick off the day, from 9 to 10 a.m. is members-only hour in the Avampato Discovery Museum galleries.

"The 'Second Saturday' was chosen for continuity and the alliteration," Menefee says. "The time was chosen to accommodate the majority of our membership, families comprised of parents with young children who are usually up early looking for something to do."

The appreciation day is marketed through the member newsletter and e-mail. Second Saturday includes drawings hourly throughout the day for items found in the center's gift shop, gift shop certificates, parking and film passes and performance tickets.

Every Second Saturday members receive a 15 percent discount on items purchased in the gift shop. The event's activities, including the drawings, are open to new members, so the day is used to promote new memberships as well.

Menefee says she's working on securing gifts for the event in advance to help promote the appreciation day in the newsletter.

The Clay Center recently merged with the Avampato Discovery Museum, which is bringing members new benefits. The monthly appreciation day allows members to experience those advantages.

Source: Missy Menefee, Membership Manager, Clay Center, Charleston, WV. Phone (304) 561-3521. E-mail: mmenefee@theclaycenter.org

91. Offer Unique Member Services

A subscription to your magazine. Recognition in the annual report. An invitation to a special reception. These are typical, albeit important, member services offered by nonprofits across the country. But if you are looking for a fresh idea, consider:

Gift of Lower-level Membership

The Lady Bird Johnson Wildflower Center (Austin, TX) offers Champion ($1,000 per year) and Sunflower Society ($1,500 per year) members the option to give the gift of a Family Level membership valued at $65. Doing so "allows our members to share their interests with friends, family or associates while increasing our membership base and furthering our message and mission," says Lori Bockstanz, annual giving manager.

Limited-edition Bronze Sculpture

The University of Arizona Alumni Association (Tucson, AZ) offers the first 100 Wildcat Family Founder ($5,000 per year) members a numbered bronze wildcat family sculpture replica of the sculpture in the university's Alumni Plaza. "This unique gift represents something that holds a special place in all Wildcat hearts," says Kelley Prust, director of membership and marketing. "The statue is only available through this special offer, which adds to the exclusivity of the membership."

Car Rental and Hotel Discounts

The Wisconsin Alumni Association (Madison, WI) offers travel-related discounts. Members can save up to 10 percent on special weekend, weekly and monthly rates, as well as up to 30 percent on thousands of hotels across the world. Offered to dues-paying members worldwide, Susan Sheehan, director of membership and new business development, says the special rates and discounts "draw great interest among our alumni members as they plan their travels and are considered an even greater bonus during today's tough economic times."

Sources: Lori Bockstanz, Annual Giving Manager, Lady Bird Johnson Wildflower Center, Austin, TX. Phone (512) 232-0137. E-mail: lbockstanz@wildflower.org
Kelley Prust, Director of Membership and Marketing, University of Arizona Alumni Association, Tucson, AZ. Phone (520) 626-9337. E-mail: prust@al.arizona.edu
Susan Sheehan, Director of Membership and New Business Development, Wisconsin Alumni Association, Madison, WI. Phone (608) 262-5895. E-mail: ssheehan@waastaff.com

92. 'Buy Here' Program Strengthens Membership

To achieve a successful membership base, it's important to support the success of each individual member. And if you can celebrate and boost your community while doing so, your efforts will have far-reaching impact.

The Iowa City Area Chamber of Commerce (Iowa City, IA) offers a "Buy Here" program that benefits both members and the Iowa City region.

Through the program, local business members are encouraged to shift five percent of their out-of-area spending to Iowa City area businesses.

Chamber officials report that this shift has created a stronger membership base while fostering a brotherhood among its 170 participating members and area business owners and strengthening the local economy.

In the first year after the implementation of the program, the Iowa City area gained back $1.1 million worth of business, chamber officials say. They anticipate the program will bring back a cumulative $95 million to the area over its duration.

"We live in a re-order world," says Rebecca Neades, vice president and director of public policy. "Sometimes there's a disconnect between a store manager and a purchasing manager."

To overcome this and relink local businesses, Neades works directly with area business owners to find local matches for business-to-business purchasing.

She notes that the program dispels the idea that local businesses cannot be competitive in bidding and pricing: "That's often a perception and not reality," she says.

Neades and her colleagues at the chamber offer the following suggestions to local business owners when aligning business purchases with the Buy Here program:

1. **Shift product purchases.** Convince members to shift purchases such as office supplies to a local vendor. Accounting for the lack of shipping costs, local vendors can be as competitive as discount suppliers.

2. **Shift service purchases.** Shift consumables such as banking, legal, accounting, 401K management, website development and hosting, public relations and more.

3. **Shift the obvious.** Consumables such as office cleaning supplies, printed materials and ad specialties are readily available locally and can be delivered without added shipping costs.

4. **Shift the subtle.** Shift your company credit card or gas card to a local bank or institution.

5. **Shift the unique.** Ask members what's unique in their business that could be purchased locally.

Neades says each participating member is asked to complete an online pledge form showing his/her support and participation in the program. This step ensures a sense of commitment to the program, she notes.

Chamber staff also heavily promote the program and include the pledge form with annual dues statements. For example, Neades says, the Buy Here program is not only addressed at each member visit, but is prominently featured at the chamber's website and in its advertising campaign.

Sources: Rebecca Neades, Vice President and Director of Public Policy; and Kelly McCann, Director of Communications, Iowa City Area Chamber of Commerce, Iowa City, IA. Phone (319) 337-9637. E-mail: rebecca@iowacityarea.com or kelly@iowacityarea.com

---

Member Talks Positively About 'Buy Here' Program

What are members of the Iowa City Area Chamber of Commerce (Iowa City, IA) saying about its "Buy Here" program?

Monica Nadeau, general manager, Coral Ridge Mall (Iowa City, IA) and a chamber member, has made a concerted effort to shift five percent of out-of-area purchases to the local region.

Doing so has been quite simple, Nadeau notes.

While she now is seeking a local vendor to supply new food trays, the first step in the mall's participation in the Buy Here program was to find a local supplier for parts and service of the mall's Zamboni machine used at its ice arena.

"We always assumed that because this is such a specialty item, we had to go through the Zamboni company," Nadeau says. "But we were able to find a local supplier for parts and service."

Nadeau has taken the effort a step further, successfully encouraging mall tenants — even those who are national retailers — to shift away from using contractors outside the region when opening a new store.

"I've been able to refer local contractors to these major retailers for bidding on construction jobs, and they've been chosen on numerous occasions because of their competitive pricing," Nadeau says. "Local contractors don't have hotel stays, travel costs and other expenses that outside contractors have to build into their bid."

With the 2008 flooding in the area, Nadeau says the Buy Here program was more important than ever as it helped with matching local business owners and residents with local providers to assist them with emergency needs.

Monica Nadeau, General Manager, Coral Ridge Mall, Coralville, IA. Phone (319) 466-1214. E-mail: monica.nadeau@gpp.com

93. Networking Opportunities Keep Members Coming Back

Want to know what current or potential benefits your members most appreciate? Ask them.

Through a member survey, staff of the Greater Fort Wayne Chamber of Commerce (Fort Wayne, IN) learned that most members join the chamber for the frequent networking opportunities it offers.

Nicole Wilkins, communications manager, says 90 percent of the chamber's 2,000 members are small business owners to whom networking is a key component to their livelihood. "Networking has become a staple to the business of a chamber," Wilkins says. "The chamber remains the place for members to network and build their business."

She cites two specific ways the chamber offers members the opportunity to hone their networking skills:

- ❏ "High Speed Networking" events in which members deliver their "elevator speech" to 21 other members within the course of an hour;
- ❏ A "Meet Me at 5" event that draws anywhere from 100 to 400 members to mingle for a bit of business while enjoying a unique venue.

To maximize the success of the events, Wilkins says, the chamber uses two critical tools to keep things running smoothly — Constant Contact (www.constantcontact.com) and WebLink (www.weblinkinternational.com).

Source: Nicole Wilkins, Communications Manager, The Greater Fort Wayne Chamber of Commerce, Fort Wayne, IN. Phone (260) 424-1435. E-mail: nwilkins@fwchamber.org

94. Looking for Benefit Ideas

Looking for new benefit ideas to offer your members? Rita Cornelius, director of membership, Greater Boerne Area Chamber of Commerce (Boerne, TX), shares two of the chamber's exceptional benefits.

"All new chamber members, with the exception of the Friend of the Chamber ($110 — Individual) and Bronze levels ($250) are offered free ads welcoming them as a new member, compliments of both local newspapers," says Cornelius.

Welcome ads are a great way to honor your newest members and let the community know about your membership growth. Cornelius details the welcome ads, saying, "In one paper is a 6 1/4 X 3 3/4-inch ad with the headline — 'Introducing the newest member of the Greater Boerne Area Chamber of Commerce courtesy of The Boerne

Star.' The second ad is in the Hill Country View with a 5 X 4-inch tall with the same caption and compliments of the Hill Country View. The members have 90 days to use the ads."

Another useful benefit offered by the chamber is complimentary mailing labels or lists produced for members' use.

"The chamber membership list is one of the best business contact tools you will find. Mailing labels or lists are available to all members at no cost," says Cornelius. All membership levels, excluding the Friend of the Chamber category, can receive one set of printed mailing labels annually at no cost. Many levels (Silver Level — $390 and above) have the ability to purchase additional sets for $100.

Source: Rita Cornelius, Director of Membership, Greater Boerne Area Chamber of Commerce, Boerne, TX. Phone (830) 249-8000. E-mail: rita@boerne.org

95. Partnerships Offer Great Member Benefits

Offer your members greater value by partnering with another organization.

The Silicon Valley Chapters of the Public Relations Society of America (PRSA-SV) and the International Association of Business Communicators (SV-IABC) partnered in January 2007.

The process to form the partnership was simple and happened in short order. The idea stemmed from the SV-IABC contacting PRSA-SV about hosting a media event together.

"It made sense. Anything that brings greater value to our members is good," Dunne says. "We're about education and professional development, advancing the PR profession and offering excellent networking opportunities."

Among the partnership goals is to co-produce future

events and workshops that would interest both organizations' members. To ensure successful attendance, the organizations are publicizing these events in advance to members. To attract members to the events, special discounts are offered.

Though the chapters cover the same geographical area, the organizations have different memberships. IABC is largely comprised of internal communications professionals, while PRSA is made up of professionals in outward-facing communications and media relations.

The partnership allows members of both organizations to share resources and expertise.

Source: Paula Dunne, President-elect, Public Relations Society of America-Silicon Valley, and President, Contos Dunne Communications, Morgan Hill, CA. Phone (408) 776-1400. E-mail: paula@contosdunne.com

96. Interest Groups Reach More Alumni, Connect Them With Organization, One Another

To reach out to more alumni, form interest groups to benefit your alumni association.

At Maryville University of St. Louis (St. Louis, MO), staff formed affinity groups to create more meaningful programming to benefit its alumni community, says Erin Verry, director of alumni relations.

"Affinity groups and programming are designed to reconnect those with shared Maryville experiences, so that they may network, socialize and support their alma mater," Verry says.

Maryville's alumni association defines affinity groups or alumni interest groups as any group of Maryville University alumni that share a common interest or like campus experience and which desires to affiliate as a sub-group of the alumni association.

Affinity groups are formed around one or more of these criteria:

- Former membership in an officially recognized student organization, such as student newspaper, fraternities/sororities and sports.
- A shared personal characteristic, including ethnicity, religion or sexual orientation.
- A common geographic location.
- A shared postgraduate professional experience, such as entrepreneurs, lawyers, common employer, etc.

Currently, the alumni association has 13 affinity groups, including ambassadors, class agents, young alumni, student alumni, various school-based advisory boards and the library board.

"We are looking to expand this list to include more student organizations, such as campus activities board, student government and honors programs," the alumni relations director says. "As the office of student life expands the number and type of student organizations, so does the alumni association."

The duties of each affinity group differs.

The affinity groups appoint a liaison to work with Maryville University Alumni Relations. The liaisons assist in:

- Reaching out to current students with the same interest or college experience.
- Communicating with prospective students.
- Assisting their groups with organization activities, such as reunions.

Affinity groups play a vital role in the overall programming goals of the alumni association.

Maryville's Alumni Association is a nonmember, non-dues organization, Verry says. "However," she adds, "affinity programming allows us to reach out to more alumni in a meaningful way that will allow them to reconnect with their alma mater and increase our alumni participation."

Sources: Erin Verry, Director of Alumni Relations; Lauren Comici, Assistant Director of Alumni Relations; Maryville University of St. Louis, St. Louis, MO. Phone (314) 529-9336. E-mail: every@maryville.edu

Ideas to Generate Alumni Support

To attract strong alumni support, start by creating an excellent student experience. That technique is paying off for Newbury College (Brookline, MA).

"We want current students to matriculate to be great alumni," says Salvadore Liberto, vice president of enrollment and dean of admissions. "The best way for this to happen is to engage current students, market to them and work to improve services for them."

Liberto offers four additional ways to create and nurture strong support from your alumni:

1. **Consider offering training programs and hiring students once they graduate.** "In our admission office, we have been able to hire some alumni as full-time staff members," Liberto says. "We learned about them as students and watched them develop in our own tour guide program, the Ambassadors. The strength of the current program provided these 'future employees' with the skill set to do the job as professionals."

2. **Prepare students for "real world" to better keep in touch with them as professionals.** "In our hotel program, for example, the fact that students have one foot in the real world as juniors or seniors provides a great transition from college," Liberto says. "The fact that they are quasi-professionals at this point makes it easier to stay connected with the school as professionals."

3. **Invite alumni back to campus to share their experiences with students.** "Our Saunders School of Hotel and Restaurant Management hosts a Leadership Day for prospective students and current students," Liberto says. "It's a huge hit, with many alumni coming back to campus to discuss their careers and the education provided here."

4. **Value feedback.** "The feedback from current students and recent alumni is extremely valuable in assessing the entire enterprise," says Liberto, "from academics to co-curricular programming, from residence life to how they view the service in financial aid."

Source: Salvadore Liberto, Vice President of Enrollment and Dean of Admission, Newbury College, Brookline, MA. Phone (617) 730-7000. E-mail: sliberto@newbury.edu

9 781118 691984